*Exploring*
Prayer

I am indebted to many writers for their wisdom and insights but in particular to Margaret Silf, John Pritchard and Stephen Cottrell. Full details of books that have shaped my thinking are given in the Bibliography. I acknowledge the influence of numerous people who have led retreats or quiet days of which I have been a part or have inspired me through their creativity – especially Angela Ashwin, Sheila Finney, Wanda Nash, Margaret Silf, Stephen Cottrell, Tim Sledge, Carol Marples, Gillian Lever and Alison White – many of whose ideas I have adapted as Prayer Exercises.

Thanks to Jacynth Hamill for help in tracing the prayer on page 49, to the children of Christ Church Primary School, Cheltenham for the prayers in chapter 2, and to 'Living Room' for their version of the Lord's Prayer in chapter 9.

Finally, thanks to all the friends who have prayed with me and for me over the years, especially my husband Tim and my sons Frank, Jonah and George.

# *Exploring* Prayer

SUE MAYFIELD

LION

A Lion Book
an imprint of
**Lion Hudson plc**
Mayfield House, 256 Banbury Road,
Oxford OX2 7DH, England
www.lionhudson.com
ISBN 978-0-7459-5237-6

First edition 2007
10  9  8  7  6  5  4  3  2  1  0

**Acknowledgments**

I am grateful to SPCK for permission to reproduce the following poems and prayers:
p. 39 'Te deum laudamus', p. 61 'The prayer of Jesus' (Lord's prayer), and p. 117
'A prayer of offering' from *Prayers and Poems* by Monica Furlong (SPCK 2004); p. 76 'For
all the sick ones' from *Praying Like a Woman* by Nicola Slee (SPCK 2004); p. 86 'May you see
Christ in others' from *The Rhythm of Life* by David Adam (SPCK 1996); and to SCM Press
for permission to include the prayer on p. 49 from *Contemporary Prayers for Public Worship*,
edited by Caryl Micklem (SCM 1967).

Thanks also to Gillian Lever and Richard Kenton Webb for permission to include the
quotations on p. 121.

pp. 12, 114 Scripture quotations are from the Good News Bible published by
The Bible Societies/HarperCollins Publishers, copyright © 1966, 1971, 1976,
1992 American Bible Society.

pp. 14–15, 30, 40, 41, 73 Scripture quotations are from the Contemporary
English Version published by The Bible Societies/HarperCollins Publishers,
copyright © 1991, 1992, 1995 American Bible Society.

pp. 20–21, 24, 25, 33, 37–38, 43, 46, 48, 50, 52, 53, 54, 66, 82, 83, 84, 85,
87, 88, 89, 92, 93, 94, 100, 102, 104, 106, 110, 113, 118 Scripture quotations taken
from the Holy Bible, New International Version, copyright © 1973, 1978, 1984
International Bible Society. Used by permission of Zondervan and Hodder &
Stoughton Limited. All rights reserved. The 'NIV' and 'New International Version'
trademarks are registered in the United States Patent and Trademark Office by
International Bible Society. Use of either trademark requires the permission of
International Bible Society. UK trademark number 1448790.

pp. 27–28, 73 Scripture quotations are from the New Revised Standard Version
published by HarperCollins Publishers, copyright © 1989 by the Division of Christian
Education of the National Council of the Churches of Christ in the USA, and are used
by permission. All rights reserved.

pp. 73, 77 Scripture quotations are from The Holy Bible, English Standard Version,
published by HarperCollins Publishers, copyright © 2001 Crossway Bibles, a division
of Good News Publishers. Used by permission. All rights reserved.

A catalogue record for this book is available
from the British Library

Typeset in 14/16 Lapidary333 BT
Printed and bound in China

# Contents

# Introduction

## Why pray?

Many people pray – in all cultures and in all faiths. Even people with no faith sometimes find themselves drawn to reach out to some bigger spiritual reality than themselves – whether simply from a sense of gratitude and wonder, or in times of trouble and distress. In the twenty-first century there is considerable interest in spirituality and a growing awareness in many people of a hunger for meaning and depth that material well-being doesn't touch. In Britain, several reality TV programmes – *Spirituality Shopper, The Monastery, Making Slough Happy, The Convent* – have identified a yearning for a deeper dimension to life and a search for purpose and peace. Philosophers and spiritual writers from numerous backgrounds have recognized this yearning for a sense of connectedness with 'the divine' as an intrinsic part of human nature. Augustine of Hippo, in the fourth century, wrote about a restlessness that he believed could only be satisfied by spending time with God.

Prayer can be part of our response to this restless longing, and a reaching into the depths of God and ourselves to find greater meaning and fulfilment in our lives.

> **'Lord, you made us for yourself and our hearts are restless until they find their rest in you.'**
>
> *Augustine of Hippo*

## What is prayer?

Prayer means many things to many people. It might be a knee-jerk reaction, a habit, a state of being, a vestige of childhood, a spontaneous outpouring of delight or concern. It may involve words or silence or the lighting of a candle.

Prayer is a reaching out beyond ourselves, a focusing of

our attention on a higher power. For Christians, prayer is at the heart of a relationship with God. It is a form of communication – the lifeline and lifeblood of faith, the means by which we express and experience the reality of God in our lives. Yet many people find prayer difficult. We may struggle to make time for it, perhaps feeling that everyone else is better at it – more effective, able to do it for longer, or more consistently.

There is an old joke that goes:

> I pray almost every day. Almost on a Monday, almost on a Tuesday… etc!

We might see prayer as a chore – as something we *ought* to do more of, like dieting or violin practice. Or as something unpalatable that we know would *do us good*, like cod liver oil. We can also attach a lot of strange and difficult words to it (some of which I'll attempt to explain and demystify in this book) – words like contrition and intercession, petition and oblation. Or we may think that we have to pray in certain ways and adopt unfamiliar patterns of speech so that we sound 'holy'. Perhaps, if faith or church is new and unfamiliar, prayer may seem as unfathomable and alien as a foreign language!

But prayer is essentially simple – as simple and as natural as breathing. It is also about *God* and not about *us*. When we focus too much on what *we* do and how *we* do it – on where we do it and how often – then we can miss the point. Prayer is about *being with God*.

## Who are we praying to?

Although prayer is common to many religions this book will focus chiefly on the Christian tradition, taking as its source the teachings of Jesus Christ and the practices of the church across the centuries.

Because prayer is essentially a relationship, we need to

'Prayer is being present to the presence of God. Prayer is the gift of ourselves to God in response to the Gifts he has given to us. Prayer is listening, loving, embracing people in God. Prayer is holding open the door of opportunity in places of despair. Prayer is struggle, joy, laughter and pain.'

*John Pritchard*

know who it is we are relating to. This book isn't primarily a book about finding God – or an introduction to the basics of Christian faith. However, if Christianity is new to you and you're not sure what kind of God Christians believe in, I hope *Exploring Prayer* will give you many insights into the God the Bible describes.

'Prayer is being loved at a deep, sweet level.'

*Richard Rohr*

The God of the Old and New Testaments is many-faceted: Creator; Rescuer; Source of Hope and Joy; Father of our Lord Jesus Christ; Judge and Defender of the poor and oppressed; Lover; Friend; Comforter; Mother who nurtures us; Shepherd who searches for us.

Because God is infinitely bigger than we are and because we – men and women alike – are made in God's image, God, of course, supersedes gender. To call God either 'he' or 'she', therefore, is limiting. But calling God 'it' makes God seem inanimate when the Bible's picture of God is quite the opposite – God is living and active, intimately concerned about our lives, mindful of human pain and tenderly seeking our company and love. In the course of this book I will refer to God as 'he', but in your own praying you

may find it helpful also to address God as 'she'.

Christians believe that we pray with Jesus and through him. When Jesus died on the cross, the temple veil, which had previously excluded ordinary people from the 'Holy of Holies' (where God was said to dwell), was ripped from top to bottom. Jesus' outstretched arms on the cross invite us into the presence of the divine.

## How to use this book

Prayer is a journey – a journey into God and a journey to the deepest, hidden levels of ourselves. To embark on a life of prayer is to begin a journey of discovery. As we grow and change, so our praying will grow and deepen too.

This book is called *Exploring Prayer*. It is – by definition – exploratory. It does not have all the answers. Nor will it do your praying for you! It will endeavour to guide you as you travel on your own journey by explaining something of what prayer is and how we might engage in it. It will – I hope –

break open the Bible's teaching on prayer and highlight some of the wisdom of the Christian tradition. It will also give you a bag-load of practical ideas for spending time in the company of the living God.

There are twenty chapters. The first nine examine the topic *What is prayer?* Chapters 10 to 20 explore different ways of praying. At the end of each chapter there are two suggested exercises or ways to pray – forty exercises in all. Try them – even if you're not sure they're quite 'you'. (You could even try one a day for the duration of Lent.) Think of these exercises as a box of tools. Some you may like and will – in future months and years – return to again and again. Others may be appropriate to particular phases of your life or specific circumstances that you find yourself in. Some of the ideas and exercises may rub you up the wrong way or leave you cold – and you'll never want to do them again. But that, too, is part of your exploration. As someone once said: 'Pray the way you can, not the way you can't.' By being open to new ways of doing things and by trying ideas that may seem strange we discover what works for us and what doesn't.

God is an awesome God whom we can never finish discovering. There is always more beauty, more mystery, more grace to find – more love, and glory, and holiness than we can imagine. And we are all different – boundlessly full of possibilities and wonderfully diverse. No two people will pray in the same way.

Because of God's riches and our own, prayer is, paradoxically, both very simple and very complex. When we turn to prayer, we respond from deep within ourselves – as a child to a loving parent. As we begin to pray we discover – in Scripture, in the world, and in two thousand years of Christian experience – a box of treasure that will take a lifetime to explore.

My own influences include Methodism, Anglicanism, the Charismatic movement, the Celtic tradition, Ignatian Spirituality and the Arts. Being a parent of three sons has helped me to integrate prayer into everyday life and to encounter God in the mess and the muddle. Working with small children and teenagers has taught me to value prayer that is tactile and hands-on. Working in a hospice has increased my awareness of the spiritual needs of people from all faiths and none. But I am not an expert. Indeed, writing a book about prayer was a daunting prospect and rarely have I employed so many delaying tactics before getting going!

In common with many people I find the older I get, the less I feel I know. So it's just as well that prayer isn't about me and my expert technique.

Archbishop of Canterbury Rowan Williams, when asked by Terry Wogan for some 'expert tips on praying', likened prayer to *sunbathing*.

> When you're lying on the beach or under the lamp,
> something is happening, something that has nothing to do
> with how you feel or how hard you're trying. You're not
> going to get a better tan by screwing up your eyes and
> concentrating. You give the time, and that's it. All you have
> to do is turn up. And then things change, at their own pace.
> You simply have to be there where the light can get at you.
>
> *PAUSE FOR THOUGHT*, RADIO 2

In the book of Revelation (the last book in the Bible) there is a poetic 'picture' of God sitting on a throne from which a life-giving stream of water is gushing. Prayer is a bit like wading into the stream.

As with the sunbathing, the important thing is that we put ourselves into the stream. Prayer is about making ourselves available to God.

Father, Mother, Lover, Friend – God invites us into his presence.

So let's step into the sunshine and wade into the stream. And don't forget, prayer is a gift.

The apostle Paul's letter to the Romans says that God's Spirit helps us to pray and prays in us:

> ...*we do not know how we ought to pray; the Spirit himself pleads with God for us in groans that words cannot express.*
> Romans 8:26

Let's receive the gift with open hands as we journey into prayer...

# PART ONE

# What is prayer?

# 1  *Encounter*

Prayer can be many things – thanksgiving, pleading, listening, wrestling, yearning, waiting – and we will explore some of these dynamics in coming chapters. But our starting point is *encounter*.

Prayer, first and foremost, is an encounter with the living God.

Exodus chapter 3 (in the Old Testament of the Bible) tells the story of Moses and a burning bush. In this powerful story, Moses has an encounter with God, who speaks to him from the midst of a blazing tree.

### *Moses and the burning bush*

*One day, Moses was taking care of the sheep and goats of his father-in-law Jethro, the priest of Midian, and Moses decided to lead them across the desert to Sinai, the holy*

*mountain. There an angel of the Lord appeared to him from a burning bush. Moses saw that the bush was on fire, but it was not burning up. 'This is strange!' he said to himself. 'I'll go over and see why the bush isn't burning up.'*

*When the Lord saw Moses coming near the bush, he called to him by name, and Moses answered, 'Here I am.*

*God replied, 'Don't come any closer. Take off your sandals — the ground where you are standing is holy. I am the God who was worshipped by your ancestors Abraham, Isaac, and Jacob.'*

*Moses was afraid to look at God, and so he hid his face.*

*The Lord said: 'I have seen how my people are suffering as slaves in Egypt, and I have heard them beg for my help because of the way they are being ill-treated. I feel sorry for them, and I have come down to rescue them from the Egyptians.*

*'I will bring my people out of Egypt into a country where there is good land, rich with milk and honey... Now go to the king! I am sending you to lead my people out of this country.'*

*But Moses said, 'Who am I to go to the king and lead your people out of Egypt?'*

*God replied, 'I will be with you. And you will know that I am the one who sent you...'*

Exodus 3:1–12

The story contains several insights about prayer.

## *Ordinary*

Moses is tending sheep when the vision occurs. Prayer breaks into our everyday lives. It isn't something apart from real life — it is at the heart of it. And it isn't something we have to do at a special time in a special place. We can meet God wherever we are, in the ordinary things we do Sunday to Saturday.

### Turning aside

Moses turns aside to look at the bush. He makes time for the encounter and gives it his attention. In the rhythm of our lives it's good to find time to 'turn aside' to prayer.

### Holy ground

God tells Moses to remove his sandals because he is standing on holy ground. Although we are invited to come freely into God's presence, we need to tread with awe and reverence and with a sense of sacred transformation.

### Belonging

God reveals himself to Moses as the God of his ancestors. Prayer starts with a relationship and with a sense of belonging.

### Self-knowledge

Moses' response to God's presence is to feel inadequate and overwhelmed. He hides his face and looks away. When they encounter God's glory, people often look inwards at themselves and see the ways in which they are not what they want to be. Chapter 6 will consider what it means to pray with an awareness of our own mistakes and brokenness.

### Purpose and promise

'My God, set me on fire.'

*Augustine of Hippo*

God gives Moses a job to do, inviting him to participate in a plan to liberate the oppressed people of Israel. (Prayer can lead us where we least expect to go!) A dialogue then takes place in which Moses grapples with his doubts and fears, and God reassures him. Prayer is a two-way conversation. Moses receives both a commission and a promise.

Prayer – as Moses discovered – can be mysterious and amazing, terrifying and life-changing, giving fresh focus and direction to our lives. Prayer can be a passionate encounter full of fiery possibilities.

## Prayer exercise: **Holy ground**

This exercise uses posture, some simple words and the action of removing our shoes to help us as we 'turn aside' to pray.

Take off your shoes and stand still and straight. (You might like to close your eyes if this helps you.)

Slowly repeat to yourself the words: *Take off your shoes. This is holy ground*.

Now adopt a posture that feels reverent – you could remain standing, sit in an upright chair, kneel or even lie face down on the floor.

Remember, wherever you are, you are in the presence of Almighty God.

Try to be very still for five minutes.

Slowly repeat to yourself Moses' words to God: *Here I am, Lord*.

## Prayer exercise: **Burning bush**

This exercise invites you to use your imagination and your senses to picture yourself in Moses' position.

Sit comfortably on a chair and close your eyes.

Imagine a mountainous desert landscape – rocks, scrubby trees, fierce sunshine. Herds of sheep and goats graze what vegetation there is.

Now picture a small tree that appears to be on fire. Walk towards it, curious.

How does it look? Describe the flames to yourself…

What does the fire sound like, and smell like?

Imagine its heat searing your skin, scorching your clothes…

Now imagine a voice addressing you from the flames. God calls your name. Hear this in your imagination…

God asks you to take off your shoes. How does the hot sand feel beneath your feet?

What posture do you adopt?

If God were to speak to you about the suffering in the world now, what images might God show you? What names of people or places would he bring to your attention? Let these images and words run through your head as you picture yourself in front of the burning bush…

Now imagine God is giving you a task to do. What might it be? How do you feel about what God is asking? Imagine a conversation between yourself and God. What pitfalls do you foresee in your own role? What reassurance might God give you?

Take as long as you want to on this encounter. Then, when you are ready, imagine yourself walking away from the fire. Where are you going now, and how do you feel? Open your eyes.

**Sit in quiet for a moment to absorb what you have experienced. You might like to write about it in a prayer journal.**

# 2  Celebration

We live in an amazing world full of wonderful things. Waterfalls, the night sky, buds opening in spring, childbirth, bird song, a field of sunflowers – even just the sun coming out on a day that has started off gloomy – can give us a feeling of well-being and make us feel glad. Expressing this gladness to God in gratitude is what we call 'thanksgiving'. This kind of prayer – a spontaneous expression of joy to God – is one of the most basic and instinctive forms of praying and comes very naturally to some people, especially children.

These prayers written by a class of nine-year-olds demonstrate this:

Dear God,
Thank you for everything in my life like my family, friends and pets.
Thank you for school and teachers, books and houses – police, traffic wardens and helpers.
Thank you for toys and games and animals like birds, cows and dogs.
Amen.

KIERAN FITZGERALD

Dear God,
Thank you so much for all these things –
for nature, birds, trees and monkeys.
Thank you for the big bright moon that glows in the night sky.
Amen.

BETHANY GARDNER

'Love all God's creation, the whole and every grain of sand in it. Love every leaf, every ray of God's light… If you love everything, you will perceive the divine mystery in things. And once you perceive it, you will begin to comprehend it better every day.'

*Dostoevsky*

Dear God,
Thank you for my mum and dad and for me.
Thank you for giving us all we need.
Thank you for food like apples and cherries.
Amen.

SOPHIA PEART

Acknowledging that good things come from God and that God is intrinsically good leads us into 'praise'. Praise, put simply, is telling God why we like him so much. Through praise we celebrate who God is and what he means to us. In thanksgiving we celebrate all that God has made and done. The book of Psalms (in the Old Testament of the Bible) is full of poems of praise and thanksgiving, and Psalm 100 is a particularly good example.

### Psalm 100

*Shout for joy to the Lord, all the earth.*
*Worship the Lord with gladness;*
*come before him with joyful songs.*
*Know that the Lord is God.*
*It is he who made us, and we are his;*
*we are his people, the sheep of his pasture.*

*Enter his gates with thanksgiving*
*and his courts with praise;*
*give thanks to him and praise his name.*

*For the Lord is good and his love endures for ever;*
*his faithfulness continues through all generations.*

Living with a sense of delight and celebration so that praise and thanksgiving spill naturally from our lips is a great antidote to cynicism, and it can help us see the positive in even the darkest situations. Having an attitude of thankfulness doesn't mean we have to be relentlessly cheerful, or paste a smile on our faces when we feel lousy (we'll focus more on how we can pray when life is tough in Chapters 6 and 7). But it does mean committing ourselves to seeing the 'diamonds in the mud' and pausing to wonder at all we take for granted. This in turn will give us a greater sense of God's presence in our world.

What are some of the things you have to celebrate in your life? A lovely thing to do, when you have an idle moment, is to make a list of your own 'seven wonders of the world', or choose your 'Desert Island Discs' (eight pieces of music that you love, plus a chosen book and a luxury item to take to your desert island). Or see if you can identify your favourite sight, sound, smell, taste and physical sensation!

**'Earth's crammed with heaven, And every common bush afire with God: But only he who sees, takes off his shoes, The rest sit round it, and pluck blackberries.'**

*Elizabeth Barrett Browning*

• • • • • • • • • • • • • • • • • • • • • • • • • • • • • • • • • • • •

**Prayer exercise: 'Chinks' of thanksgiving**

This exercise uses glass beads – the sort you can buy quite cheaply in candle or home décor shops. As an alternative you could use a bag of children's marbles.

Sit comfortably on the floor or on a low chair and place a glass bowl within easy reach. In another container put glass beads or marbles.

Think about your life and the things you are thankful for – people who are special to you, favourite food or places, elements of work or leisure that give you joy, good experiences you have had or anticipate having.

Move slowly from one item to another and for each thing that comes to mind, pick up a glass bead, hold it and then drop it into the glass bowl.

Enjoy the 'chink' sound of glass on glass and offer this to God as an 'audio thank you'. You could use the following prayer to conclude the exercise:

**Thank you, generous God,
for all your good gifts.
Let these 'chinks' of gratitude
give pleasure to you,
as all these things have given pleasure to me.
Amen.**

• • • • • • • • • • • • • • • • • • • • • • • • • • • • • • • • • • • • • •

## Prayer exercise: **Psalm of praise**

This exercise involves writing your own appreciation of God. You will need a sheet of paper and a pen or pencil. (As a preparation you might like to read some more of the Psalms. Numbers 103, 105, 106, 113, 117 and 146 are especially good ones.)

On a sheet of paper, jot down ten words that describe what you think God is like.

Now make a list of some of the things God has done.

Arrange these words and ideas into a psalm of your own.

You might want to use repeated phrases such as 'God, I praise you because…' or 'You, Lord, are…' or (as in Psalm 103) 'Praise the Lord, O my soul…'.

When you are happy with what you have written, read it aloud to God.

# 3  *Awareness*

In Chapter 1, we considered prayer as an encounter with God, and in Chapter 2, the aspect of prayer we call praise and thanksgiving. In Chapters 4 to 8 we will explore more aspects of praying but first let us look at what many spiritual writers have called 'practising the presence'.

All prayer – whatever form it takes – is about an awareness of the presence of God. If we didn't have *some* sense of a divine being in us and around us, prayer would merely be talking to ourselves.

'Practising the presence' involves holding two things in tension:

- Prayer is about consciously seeking God's presence – 'turning aside' as Moses did to contemplate the burning bush (Chapter 1) or 'entering his courts with thanksgiving', like the Psalmist (Chapter 2). It involves deliberate actions and practices.

- But prayer is also about developing an awareness that God is already present in our lives and our world. It involves 'tuning in' to what God is doing and saying.

Prayer, therefore, as well as being something that we *do*, is something that we *are* – it's an attitude of life.

The ripping apart of the temple veil at the moment of Jesus' death (mentioned already on page 9) symbolizes the end of a divide between God and humanity, secular and sacred, natural and supernatural. In Jesus, God is made fully present on the earth. Holy God is embodied and 'fleshed-out' – or 'incarnate' as Christians put it. Heaven and earth are forever merged and mingled so that God's presence is above us, beneath us, beside us and within us.

As we pray, we attune ourselves to this presence. Praying people are a bit like satellite dishes on the sides of houses,

> 'To be with God wondering, that is adoration. To be with God gratefully, that is thanksgiving. To be with God ashamed, that is contrition. To be with God with others on our heart, that is intercession. The secret is the quest for God's presence; "Thy face Lord will I seek." '
>
> *Michael Ramsey*

their eager faces upturned to the skies. All satellite dishes do is face in the right direction and receive messages. Like the sunbather in Rowan Williams' image of prayer (quoted in the Introduction), the important thing is being there; being in a place (literally and metaphorically) where we can receive the 'satellite images' or the 'sun's rays'.

Being a satellite dish – or indeed, sitting in the sun – sounds quite easy. Perhaps we sometimes try too hard when it comes to prayer. Perhaps we need simply to grasp that – however we feel – God is with us and within us. As Woody Allen puts it, 'Eighty per cent of success is just showing up!'

So how can we become more aware of the presence of God? How can we 'practise the presence'?

The Psalmist suggests the key is in stillness.

> *Be still, and know that I am God.*
> Psalm 46:10

There is a story of a group of porters, hired for an expedition by a party of Europeans, who – being made to rush through the jungle at a ridiculous pace – sat down in a clearing and refused to go any further, saying this: 'We've come so far and so fast that now we have to wait for our souls to catch up with us!'

As a culture, we are more fast-moving than ever and many of us have no idea how to be still and do 'nothing'.

The Indian poet Tagore wrote:

> Sit still, my heart, do not raise your dust...
> RABINDRANATH TAGORE

How can we help our hearts to sit still? What can we do to let the dust of agitation settle?

The following exercise is designed to help you 'be still' with God. Don't worry if you don't manage to be still the

'Prayer is not primarily saying words or thinking thoughts. It is, rather, a stance. It's a way of living *in* the Presence, living in *awareness* of the Presence, and... of enjoying the Presence.'

*Richard Rohr*

first time you try it. Stillness is a skill to be learned – like riding a bike or playing a musical instrument. The more often you do it, the easier it will become.

Think of your first attempt as simply creating space – like hacking down trees to make a clearing in a forest. The more space you make, the more the light can penetrate.

And remember that God enjoys your company as much as you enjoy God's.

> *For the Lord takes delight in his people.*
> Psalm 149:4

• • • • • • • • • • • • • • • • • • • • • •

## Prayer exercise:
# Be still

The purpose of this exercise is to practise being still. Don't worry if you don't *feel* anything. Just relax, and enjoy doing nothing in the presence of God!

Sit comfortably on a straight-backed chair with your legs uncrossed and your feet on the floor.

Rest your hands in your lap and try to be as relaxed as possible.

Concentrate on your breathing – in and out – your chest rising and falling. Try to breathe deeply and easily, and imagine that any tension and anxiety are leaving your body as you breathe out.

Now focus your attention on each part of your body in turn from the ground upwards – feet, legs, back, hands, arms, neck, face and scalp. Imagine each part of you becoming

relaxed and still, and any tension slipping from you.

When you feel relaxed, begin to say the following prayer. Say it a line at a time and leave a pause between each line to let the words sink in.

> Be still and know that I am God.
> Be still and know that I am.
> Be still and know.
> Be still.
> Be.

• • • • • • • • • • • • • • • • • • • • • • • • • • • • • • • • • • • • •

## Prayer exercise: **Patrick's breastplate**

This exercise invites you to say an ancient Celtic prayer using posture and movement.

Stand in a space big enough to stretch out your arms.

For each of the five lines of this prayer there are gestures to help you 'feel' the impact of the words. Say the prayer aloud, slowly – allowing time to do each movement without rushing.

| | |
|---|---|
| **God above me** | *Reach up high and turn your palms upwards as if lifting up the sky* |
| **God beneath me** | *Crouch down and put your hands on the floor* **or** *Remain standing and extend your arms downwards, turning your palms towards the floor* |
| **God before me** | *Stretch your arms out in front of you and turn your hands up at the wrist as if pressing against an invisible wall* |
| **God behind me** | *Reach behind you and turn your hands as if pressing against a wall that runs parallel to your back* |
| **God within me.** | *Bend your arms at the elbows and cross them over your chest, like a breastplate* |

Repeat this several times until it feels familiar.

# 4 *Ask, seek, knock*

As a child I remember being told by reproachful adults, 'I want never gets!' Perhaps this was a necessary curb to brattishness but it is – for all that – completely untrue. The truth is often quite the opposite: those who want things most are most likely to make things happen, most inclined to make dreams come true.

Wanting things is OK. In fact, as the seventeenth-century poet Thomas Traherne writes, *wanting* is deeply good:

> Wants are the bands and cements between God and us…
> From eternity it was requisite that we should want. We
> could never else have enjoyed anything: our own wants are
> treasures.
>
> THOMAS TRAHERNE

Jesus told a story about wanting and asking which is recorded in Luke chapter 11.

> *'Suppose one of you has a friend, and you go to him at midnight and say to him, "Friend, lend me three loaves of bread, for a friend of mine has arrived, and I have nothing to set before him."*
>
> *'And he answers from within, "Don't bother me; the door has already been locked and my children are with me in bed; I cannot get up and give you anything." I tell you, even though he will not get up and give him anything because he is his friend, at least because of his persistence he will get up and give him whatever he needs.*
>
> *'So I say to you, ask, and it will be given to you; search, and you will find; knock, and the door will be opened for you. For everyone who asks receives, and everyone who searches finds, and for everyone who*

knocks, the door will be opened. Is there anyone among you who, if your child asks for a fish, will give a snake instead of a fish? Or if the child asks for an egg, will give a scorpion? If you then, who are evil, know how to give good gifts to your children, how much more will the heavenly Father give the Holy Spirit to those who ask him?'

Luke 11:5–13

People have often misinterpreted this story, thinking that it somehow suggests that God is fundamentally mean and disinterested and that prayer is nothing more than nagging – we badger a grudging God until he listens to our requests in order to shut us up! But the key to this story – and to a similar story that Jesus told in Luke 18:2–5 where a desperate widow pesters a corrupt judge into giving her justice – is in the phrase '*How much more* will God…' What is important is the *contrast* between God and the characters in the story. God is *not* like the groggy, reluctant friend at midnight, or the hard-hearted judge. He is like a loving, generous parent. If even the hungry friend and the abused widow eventually got a response to their requests, *how much more* will God turn a listening ear to the wants and needs of his children.

God, as our Father, wants us to come to him with the things that concern us. He wants us – with the simplicity and trust of a child – to expect an audience as we come to him with our yearnings and our restlessness about all that is not as it should be. This involves both believing that God is good and being prepared to lower some of the barriers we erect around ourselves as adults.

What, then, do you want? Really want?

The things we want often reveal a great deal about what we are like under the surface – or indeed on it! This very honest reflection about prayer written by a young British woman recognizes the shallowness of the things she longs for and the ways in which she has been shaped by a culture of advertising:

> My prayers are knee-jerks – material and often selfish.
> Like many of my contemporaries, I'm a sucker for the instant results the commercials promise me.
> I believe that a certain perfume will make me desirable, a certain drink will make me more popular, a certain watch will make me seem distinctive.
> I don't pray for world peace or global justice.
> I pray that the dress I like will be in the sale, I pray that there will be a parking space outside the salon, I pray that it will be sunny on Saturday.
> RACHEL

In what ways have your own longings been shaped by the culture in which you live? What are your deepest wants and how can you express these to God the Father?

The following prayer exercises invite you to get in touch with your wants and to knock, with an expectation that doors will be opened.

• • • • • • • • • • • • • • • • • • • • • • • • • • • • • • • • • •

## Prayer exercise: **Prayer beads**

This exercise involves identifying the things we yearn for most and then using threaded beads as an aide to prayer. For this you will need five beads (ideally, all different) and some string or threading elastic. (Buy beads from a craft shop or recycle an old necklace. Alternatively you could make some beads from air-hardening clay – poke a hole through the middle with a matchstick before they are dry.)

Think of *five* things you really want. These things may be personal (for example, you may want to rediscover a sense of joy you feel you've lost;

'We are in God's family, and we matter to him. So don't tiptoe into God's presence, trying to find the secret of attracting his attention. Just say "Hello, Father," and know that he loves to hear your voice…'

*Bill Hybels*

you may long for a more fulfilling job; you may yearn for a partner or a child), or they may involve the people you love (wanting your friend's marriage to be repaired; wanting your mother's illness to be cured), or they may be more global (wanting a peace settlement to be achieved in Israel–Palestine; wanting justice for political prisoners; and so on).

Now thread your five beads onto a piece of string or elastic and knot the ends or tie them onto your wrist as a band. The five beads are going to symbolize your five 'wants', so decide which one is going to be which.

Hold the beads one at a time and reflect on the thing you have identified yourself as wanting. Tell God about your wants in your own words.

● ● ● ● ● ● ● ● ● ● ● ● ● ● ● ● ● ● ● ● ● ● ● ● ● ● ● ● ● ● ● ● ● ● ● ● ● ● ● ● ● ● ● ● ● ●

## Prayer exercise: **Knock knock**

As with the previous exercise, this exercise invites you to identify and articulate your wants to God. It incorporates the physical act of knocking to help you reflect on Jesus' words, **'Knock, and the door will be opened for you.'**

It also explores the idea of Jesus knocking on the door of our lives. Revelation 3:20 says, '**Listen! I am standing and knocking at your door…'**

The exercise centres around four questions with a repeated phrase and accompanying action following each question. Take as long as you like over the exercise.

Sit or stand within easy reach of a wooden table or door that you can knock on.

● Ask yourself: *What is the one thing I would most like God to do in the world?* (Think about your answer silently or express it aloud in your own words.)
Now knock on the door or table: [*Knock knock knock*]
Say aloud, **'Knock, and the door will be opened.'**

● Ask yourself: *What single thing do I most need right now?*
[*Knock knock knock*]
**'Knock, and the door will be opened.'**

● Ask yourself: *What gift do I most want God to give me?*
  *[Knock knock knock]*
  **'Knock, and the door will be opened.'**

● Consider: *God wants to inhabit and transform every part of your life.*
  Invite God, in your own words, to make a home in you.
  *[Knock knock knock]*
  **'Knock, and the door will be opened.'**

# 5  *Listening*

I wonder if you have ever had a relationship with someone that felt a bit 'one-sided'? Perhaps you made all the running, did all the talking, and the friend seemed negligent or disinterested. Or alternatively the friend was self-absorbed, talking all the time about their needs and concerns, and you felt overlooked and invisible.

We have said already that prayer is a relationship. Healthy relationships are two-way – mutual and balanced – not one-sided. Prayer then should be a two-way conversation where we make time to *listen* to God rather than just talking.

But how can we listen to God? Rarely do we 'hear' God with the clarity of a human voice. Indeed, we often associate claims of 'hearing voices' with deranged behaviour. (The man who shot John Lennon, for example, claimed he had 'heard God's voice'.) How can we hear God without compromising our sanity? And how can we know that what we hear is authentic and is not just our mind making things up? Does listening to God always involve words?

Many Christians believe God 'speaks' to them through words, either the words of others – a sermon or a conversation with a friend – or the words of the Bible. We call the Bible 'the Word of God' and believe that, through it, God communicates his will and his priorities to us. Certain stories or passages from the Bible may suddenly seem to light up and 'jump out at us' in particular circumstances as if God were communicating something specific.

But God's voice may also be wordless. God may 'speak' through the beauty of the created world. A sudden burst of light through the trees illuminating our path may assure us of God's guiding presence. Frost on a spider's web may speak to us about the precariousness of our planet and the need to treat it with care, or about the value and beauty of small everyday tasks. Sometimes in the midst of a difficult decision or a complex situation we may have a deep sense of peace or 'rightness' that seems to come from God. The eighteenth-century founder of the Methodist movement, John Wesley, once wrote about his heart feeling 'strangely warmed'. We need to

listen, not only to our minds, but also to the feelings and stirrings of our emotional selves as we focus our attention on God.

This story from the first book of Kings in the Old Testament describes the prophet Elijah listening out for God.

*And the word of the Lord came to him: 'What are you doing here, Elijah?'*

*He replied, 'I have been very zealous for the Lord God Almighty. The Israelites have rejected your covenant, broken down your altars, and put your prophets to death with the sword. I am the only one left, and now they are trying to kill me, too.'*

*The Lord said, 'Go out and stand on the mountain in the presence of the Lord, for the Lord is about to pass by.'*

*Then a great and powerful wind tore the mountains apart and shattered the rocks before the Lord, but the Lord was not in the wind. After the wind there was an earthquake, but the Lord was not in the earthquake. After the earthquake came a fire, but the Lord was not in the fire. And after the fire came a gentle whisper. When Elijah heard it, he pulled his cloak over his face and went and stood at the mouth of the cave.*

*Then a voice said to him, 'What are you doing here, Elijah?'*

1 Kings 19:9–13

Earlier in the story Elijah has been involved in a spectacular display of God's power (you can read the story in 1 Kings 18:16–39). Now he is dejected, exhausted and full of self-pity. Fleeing for his life, he makes his way to the mountain to hear God. Perhaps Elijah is expecting God to make another dramatic appearance – address him from the earthquake, or the furious wind, or the raging fire. But this time God's voice comes as a gentle whisper. (Some translations of the Bible call this 'a still, small voice'.)

Elijah hears God when the noise subsides and all is quiet. In our own praying we are more likely to hear God's side of the dialogue if we learn to silence the noise – both the noise outside us and the noise inside.

We live in an extraordinarily noisy world. Rarely are we allowed to be silent. Even in lifts, or when we are waiting on the phone, music is pumped out at us.

In his book *The Screwtape Letters,* C. S. Lewis imagines the devil trying to banish both music and silence from the world and filling it, instead, with noise. Screwtape (the devil) writes to his apprentice nephew anticipating the deadening, dehumanizing effect blanket noise will have – blunting consciences and drowning out the things that really matter.

… noise which alone defends us from silly qualms, despairing scruples, and impossible desires. We will make the whole universe a noise in the end.

C. S. LEWIS

The type of prayer that we call 'listening' requires us to get beneath the surface din of our everyday lives into the quiet depths of silence. This is a bit like going underwater – leaving behind the choppy, splashy surface and going into the calm underneath. The following exercises are designed to help you practise 'going underwater' where you can be still and be open to God. Don't be surprised if you find this difficult. And don't expect instant results.

You may discover that sitting still and 'doing nothing' makes you drowsy and you nod off. Or you may find that your mind goes into over-drive and you easily become distracted. You think of jobs you haven't done, or a comment someone made, or you find that a tune you heard hours ago on the car radio suddenly goes round and round your head and won't stop! One way of handling these distractions is to keep a notebook by you to jot down things that require action later. Or try using thoughts that pop into

'The lover of silence draws close to God. He talks to Him in secret and God enlightens him.'

*John Climacus*

your head as springboards for prayer. If, for example, you suddenly remember that there is someone you must ring, say a brief prayer for that person and then turn your attention back to listening and stillness.

In the quiet, you are making space for God to speak. You are – as the writers of the Psalms often put it – 'seeking God's face'.

But how, having achieved some measure of stillness, can we be certain that what we 'hear' is from God and is not just our own ideas or wish-fulfilment?

Ask yourself this:

● Is this thought compatible with what I know of God's character and purposes from reading the Bible or does it seem at odds with this?

● Is this thought good and life-giving, focusing my attention on others, God and Creation rather than on myself?

Finally, what if you don't hear anything at all? Remember the satellite dishes in Chapter 3? All they do is point in the right direction and wait for a signal. God isn't a vending machine, programmed to give us whatever we want if only we get the right coin in the right slot. He is Almighty God, mysterious and unfathomable – raging fire and still, small voice. If God seems silent or if you feel 'deaf' today, come again tomorrow.

The poet Gerard Manley Hopkins wrote:

> For I greet him the days I meet him,
> And bless when I understand.

●●●●●●●●●●●●●●●●●●●●●●●●●●●●●●●●●●●●●●●●●●●

Prayer exercise: **Speak, Lord, I'm listening...**

This exercise builds on the 'Be still' exercise in Chapter 3. (You might like to do that exercise first to make yourself relaxed and 'centred'.)

It uses words based on what the prophet Samuel said to God as a small child – 'Speak Lord, your servant is listening.' (You can read about this in 1 Samuel 3:1–10.)

Sit very still in an upright chair with your feet on the floor. Still yourself by focusing on your breathing and relaxing each part of your body in turn (see page 25).

Ask God to direct your thoughts.

Say aloud the words, 'Speak, Lord, I'm listening…'

Now focus your attention on God. Try to keep your mind still so that it doesn't go 'off track', but be kind to yourself – if you find your mind wandering, acknowledge the thoughts in your head (however banal) and use them as a springboard to 'bounce' your attention back to God.

Try to be quiet and focused for five minutes.

You might like to write down anything you felt God 'said' to you so that you can think further about it.

• • • • • • • • • • • • • • • • • • • • • • • • • • • • • • • • •

## Prayer exercise: **Eagles' wings**

This exercise introduces a passage of the Bible in which God promises to renew the strength of the weary so that they will feel as if they are riding on the backs of eagles. Use the Bible passage to focus your thoughts on God's empowering presence.

Sit still or lie on the floor. Become aware of your breathing and try to be as relaxed as you can. If you are sitting, imagine your hands becoming heavy in your lap. If you are lying down, imagine you are sinking heavily through the floor.

If you are feeling weary or burdened in any way, picture this tiredness or worry leaving you now.

When you feel relaxed, read the following words from Isaiah 40. (If you are doing this as a group exercise get one person to read this aloud while the others keep their eyes closed.)

> Do you not know?
> Have you not heard?
> The Lord is the everlasting God,
> the Creator of the ends of the earth.

He will not grow tired or weary,

and his understanding no-one can fathom.

He gives strength to the weary and increases the power of the weak.

Even youths grow tired and weary, and young people stumble
and fall;

but those who hope in the Lord will renew their strength.

They will soar on wings like eagles;

they will run and not grow weary,

they will walk and not be faint.

Isaiah 40:28–31

Let these words about tiredness and new energy absorb your thoughts. Close your eyes and picture an eagle soaring. Picture someone running tirelessly. Ask yourself:

● What does this passage say to me, here, now?
● What messages does it contain for me or my family or for situations –
   global or personal – that are concerning me?

Let your mind free-wheel – like an eagle riding air currents – and see where it takes you.

Now open your eyes and thank God for any new insights you have been given.

# 6 *Lamenting and penitence*

So far in this book we have focused largely on prayer that is positive: coming to God with a sense of wonder and thanksgiving; coming with joyful praise and with an expectation of blessing and care.

But what about the times when we feel more negative – when we are angry or sad or low? What about the times when life deals harshly with us – when we experience the death of a loved one, serious illness, the loss of a job, the breakdown of a relationship? How can we pray *then*? And how can we pray in those moments when doubt clouds our picture and God seems far off – when we are struggling to make sense of our faith, when the dots just won't join up?

Writer Monica Furlong expresses the difficulty of praising God when we are suffering:

> **Te deum laudamus**
> Yes, we do, or I do.
> It's not difficult.
> The world's worth praising.
> Its creator
> By no means hard to love.
> Only I find pain difficult,
> Not in a niggling 'Problem of Pain' sort of way,
> But because when I am in pain
> He ceases to exist.
> Deus absconditus
> How do I praise you?
> MONICA FURLONG

This chapter will try to give some insights into how we might pray when we feel we *can't* pray, and some ideas of what – prayerfully – to do with our negative emotions. It will also address the form of prayer we call 'penitence' –

being sorry for the ways in which we and others have messed up God's world and failed to live as God intended.

The book of Psalms, the ancient prayer book of the Jews, is essential reading when life is tough or we find ourselves in misery and despair. These verses powerfully express isolation, sorrow, frustration and desperation.

*Why are you far away, Lord?*
*Why do you hide yourself when I am in trouble?*
Psalm 10:1

*My groaning has worn me out.*
*At night my bed and pillow are soaked with tears.*
Psalm 6:6

*How much longer, Lord, will you forget about me?*
*Will it be forever? How long will you hide?*
*How long must I be confused and miserable all day?*
Psalm 13:1–2

*Day and night my tears are my only food,*
*as everyone keeps asking 'Where is your God?'*
Psalm 42:3

*My God, my God, why have you deserted me?*
*Why are you so far away?*
*Won't you listen to my groans and come to my rescue?*
*I cry out day and night, but you don't answer,*
*and I can never rest.*
Psalm 22:1–2

'It's companions like these that we need when our world is falling apart. We need friends in low places, people who have entered the darkness and spoken quietly of how they survived.'

*John Pritchard*

In hard times the Psalms can be like 'companions'.

The writers of the Psalms don't hold back from crying out to God. They bring him their anger, their outrage, their pain, their sense of injustice. All human emotions are valid in prayer. There is no need to tiptoe politely with God – to pretend that all is well when it is not – or to conceal the depths of our feelings in order to 'spare God's blushes'! God

wants us to be real and to come as we are, whatever our state of confusion and turmoil.

These two short prayers written by young people address God very honestly:

Good God,
where are you?
How can you leave
the world in such a mess?
If you exist
then DO SOMETHING!
Amen.

I'm angry, Lord.
My hands are dirty.
My heart is bleeding.
Look me in the eyes
and tell me God is love.

Several of the Psalms talk about tears. In our culture we are often rather suspicious of expressions of emotion —

especially in public worship – but in the Middle Ages, 'spiritual weeping' was greatly valued and mystic writers wrote of 'The Gift of Tears'.

There is a strange story in the Old Testament, in the book of Genesis (32:22–32). Jacob, who has already cheated his brother out of his birthright and deceived his dying father, spends an extraordinary night in the desert wrestling with an angel. Jacob and the angel grapple violently until dawn, when Jacob says, 'I will not let you go until you bless me!' When daylight comes, Jacob is wounded but blessed.

There are times in life when we may feel as if we are in a wrestling bout and our prayer consists of nothing more than

clinging on. Spiritual writers sometimes call these bleak and desolate periods of life 'desert times', because it can feel as if we are in the wilderness.

Once, when I was going through a difficult and sad time, a friend gave me a hot water bottle and encouraged me to sit and cuddle it and to think of God as a source of comfort. Clutching the warmth as I sat silently was about as close to prayer as I could get at that moment. But it *was* prayer. I was in God's company and God was sustaining me – whether it felt like it or not.

Sometimes the phases of life when we suffer are the times when we 'grow' personally and spiritually. To say this is always so would be glib, but *sometimes* our experience of what has often been called 'the Dark Night of the Soul' can be creative.

What, though, of the kind of pain that comes from regret and an awareness of our own mistakes and failure? What about suffering that is of our own making – that is a consequence of our weakness or malice or selfishness? How can we pray when we feel wretched and sorry? How can we bring our broken, messy lives to God in prayer?

Again the Psalms are helpful. King David, after a chain of events including adultery, trickery and assassination, cries out to God for mercy and forgiveness:

*Have mercy on me, O God, according to your unfailing love... wash away all my iniquity and cleanse me from my sin... against you, you only, have I sinned and done what is evil in your sight.*
Psalm 51:1–2, 4

Christians believe that, because of the death of Jesus, we can come to God – however dirty our hands and however stained our consciences – and receive his grace and forgiveness. All that

'Every child comes to birth through the real agony of labour through which the mother must live... A great deal of human suffering is unnecessary and destructive, and can and should be resisted and alleviated. Yet it remains true that each individual's personal experience of pain can sometimes be labour pain...'

*Margaret Silf*

'Weeping is a gentle release of water that washes, baptizes, and renews. Weeping leads to owning our complicity in a problem. Weeping is the opposite of blaming and also the opposite of denying. It leads to deep healing when inspired by the Spirit.'

*Richard Rohr*

matters is that we are sorry and that we embrace the new start God gives us.

In the Old Testament, the Jews would often do things outwardly to symbolize that they were sorry for personal or collective wrongs. They would put ashes on their heads and tear their clothing as signs of penitence. God wants us to be sorry for wrong we have done, not because he wants to make us feel bad, but because genuine sorrow for mistakes – expressed in penitence – can lead to healing and freedom. When we say 'sorry', we crack through the crust of pride and self-righteousness that keeps us from God and from one another and move into a deeper place of encounter.

● ● ● ● ● ● ● ● ● ● ● ● ● ● ● ● ● ● ● ● ● ● ● ● ● ● ● ● ● ● ● ● ● ● ● ●

## Prayer exercise: **Bowl of tears**

Psalm 56:8 says that God has collected our tears and stored them tenderly. This exercise uses this idea of a bowl of tears that God sees and values, and encourages us to name in prayer the things that trouble and grieve us. Use a large bowl or bucket for the exercise, or better still – if you are able – use a pond or river.

Find a collection of small pebbles. (If you don't have access to an outdoor source use gravel from a garden centre or the kind of polished ornamental stones that home furnishing stores often stock.)

Sit or kneel beside a bowl or bucket filled with water – or (if you are doing this outdoors) stand beside a pond or river.

Think of the things that make you sad or angry. These may be personal (the illness of a friend, bereavement, unemployment) or they may be global (poverty, flood damage, HIV). Be honest about the questions these issues raise.

Name each thing aloud to God and, as you do so, drop (or throw) a pebble into the water. Watch the stones splash and then sink. Know that God hears each concern and notices each tear.

Take as long as you like over this. You may like to conclude with the words:

O Lord, hear my prayer.

● ● ● ● ● ● ● ● ● ● ● ● ● ● ● ● ● ● ● ● ● ● ● ● ● ● ● ● ● ● ● ● ● ● ● ●

## Prayer exercise: **Lord, have mercy**

This prayer exercise uses the Jewish idea of torn garments as a sign of penitence. Ripping and shredding tissue paper replaces the action of tearing cloth but the symbolism of sorrowful tearing is still there.

You will need several sheets of tissue paper (not toilet tissue but the crackly kind of tissue paper you can get in gift or craft shops) – ideally in a variety of colours.

Sit at a table or on the floor surrounded by untorn sheets of tissue paper.

Bring to mind things for which you are sorry. These may include personal mistakes or attitudes, or more communal, global things such as failure to protect the planet, indifference to poverty or aggressive self-interest by one nation at another's expense. (You might like to make a list of some of these things to guide your prayers.)

Name these things to God slowly – either in your own words or using the wording: *Lord, I am sorry for…*

As you name each thing take a piece of paper and tear it slowly – letting the shredded fragments fall in a heap.

You could conclude your prayers with these words which are known as the *Kyrie* (*Kyrie* is Greek for 'Lord, have mercy'):

Lord, have mercy. Christ, have mercy. Lord, have mercy.

Keep your scraps of torn tissue for the 'Prayer bowls' exercise in Chapter 20. By recycling them they become a symbol of the way God uses even our mistakes and failures creatively.

# 7  *Carrying and holding*

In the previous chapter we explored ways in which we can bring honest doubt, sorrow and dismay to God and express emotions such as sadness and regret in our prayers. In this chapter we take a step further to think about how we can pray meaningfully and constructively for people and situations that touch and concern us.

There is a lovely story at the beginning of Mark's Gospel about four people who carry their paralyzed friend to Jesus on a stretcher. Arriving at the crowded house where Jesus is, they find that the only way to gain access to him is by lowering their friend down through the roof.

> *A few days later, when Jesus again entered Capernaum, the people heard that he had come home. So many gathered that there was no room left, not even outside the door, and he preached the word to them.*
>
> *Some men came, bringing to him a paralytic, carried by four of them. Since they could not get him to Jesus because of the crowd, they made an opening in the roof above Jesus and, after digging through it, lowered the mat the paralyzed man was lying on. When Jesus saw their faith he said to the paralytic, 'Son, your sins are forgiven.'*
>
> Mark 2:1–5

The friends go to considerable lengths to get their friend to Jesus. Perhaps they aren't sure exactly what Jesus will do – or how he'll do it – when they get there but they take the risk, believing that bringing their suffering friend into Jesus' presence will somehow be good and life-giving. Jesus is impressed by their faith. He heals the paralyzed man, telling him to pick up his mat and walk, but he also addresses the man's deeper spiritual needs by telling him his sins are forgiven.

Praying for the needs of others – what Christians sometimes call 'intercession' – is rather like the action of the four men. We carry those we love, those whose pain we feel, to the feet of Jesus. It doesn't matter if we don't know what will happen next, or if we can't see what our friends need most and how God will ever meet that need. We simply carry them, trusting in God's goodness.

If – as we said in the Introduction – prayer is a bit like sunbathing, then intercession is like gathering up those we care about and taking them to the seaside so that they, too, can be bathed in the life and light of the sun.

Intercession literally means pleading on someone else's behalf. When we pray, we are saying: 'Lord there's this situation I'm concerned about…' This kind of praying will often involve pain for us. The former Archbishop of Canterbury Michael Ramsey wrote this:

> The praying Christian draws inspiration from the world. Sometimes the beauty he sees in the world will stir him to wonder and worship… More often perhaps the agony of the world will draw him to the compassion of Jesus and stir his will to pray.

> 'So much is happening on earth that cannot be fixed or explained, but it can be felt and suffered. I think a Christian is one who, along with Jesus, agrees to feel, to suffer the pain of the world.'
>
> *Richard Rohr*

Compassion means 'feeling with'. Allowing ourselves to be touched by other people's suffering is a necessary starting point for this kind of prayer. In his letter to the Romans the apostle Paul writes:

> *Rejoice with those who rejoice; mourn with those who mourn.'*
> Romans 12:15

Sometimes in mourning with those who mourn we will have a profound sense of powerlessness.

In the next chapter we will consider the question of what actually happens when we pray – whether in fact things can be 'fixed' by prayer – but for now, let us stay with the image of carrying people to Jesus.

If intercessory prayer involves laying ourselves open to the sufferings of the world it can also mean taking action to alleviate those sufferings. Healing for the paralyzed man entailed a certain amount of action from his friends. They had to put themselves out quite a lot – carry him on his mat, painstakingly (and perhaps embarrassingly) dismantle a roof, find ropes, risk the humiliation of other people's anger. Praying for the needs of others may involve us in action too. In the story in the Gospels that we call 'the Feeding of the 5,000' (Luke 9:10–17) Jesus' disciples come to him to report that many people are hungry. Jesus' response is blunt: 'Feed them, then!' Sometimes when we pray whole-heartedly for others we will find ourselves being asked to be part of the answer to our prayer.

Praying may involve us in struggle and in political action. Praying for peace, for example, may involve us in fighting for justice.

The Corrymeela Community, who have for many years worked for reconciliation between Protestants and Catholics in Northern Ireland, recognize that peace is not just the absence of trouble but is also the struggle to resolve differences and connect divided lives. This prayer has been used by the Corrymeela Community:

Show us, good Lord,
the peace we should seek,
the peace we must give,
the peace we can keep,
the peace we must forgo,
And the peace you have given in Jesus Christ our Lord.

TAKEN FROM *CONTEMPORARY PRAYERS FOR PUBLIC WORSHIP*

But how can we carry the hurting people and places of the world to God – feeling their pain as Jesus feels it – without being overwhelmed by the misery and abuse we encounter all around us? How can we pray without completely losing our own peace of mind? There is so much pain in the world, we cannot possibly engage meaningfully with *all* of it in our prayers.

The prayer exercise on page 51 invites you to pray as you watch the TV evening news. But what if you find that too overwhelming? And how can you avoid 'compassion fatigue'?

You might find it useful to focus on one particular item of news, one particular face or one individual person's story. A story is told of hundreds of beached starfish lying on the shore. Moved to do something to help, a woman, passing by, picked up one starfish and carried it back into the sea. Someone challenged the woman, pointing out the futility of her action. 'What difference does it make to the situation if you throw *one* back?' The woman replied, 'It makes every difference to *that* starfish!' The four men in the story carried just one friend. There were probably hundreds of others in Capernaum who needed Jesus that day but they couldn't carry everybody. Let's not let the scale of the world's need stop us from carrying *some* of that need to God in prayer. We *can* carry a hurting friend, a sick neighbour, a bereaved relative, a depressed colleague, or that one face that touches us as we watch the news. And we can do it in the belief that God loves the person we carry even more than *we* do and that Jesus, on the cross, holds and knows that person's pain.

Often in our prayers of intercession we won't know what

'Teresa of Avila reminds us that [Jesus] has no hands on earth but ours, no eyes, no limbs but ours. If we ask him to act on behalf of others we must be willing to become the implements of that action. Perhaps our reluctance to do so is the reason why so many of our intercessions seem to remain unanswered.'

*Margaret Silf*

to say. We will simply bring people to Jesus. We may 'hold' them as we would hold a distressed child – wordlessly tender – perhaps using our imagination to visualize this holding. The following prayer exercise helps us to think more about this idea.

• • • • • • • • • • • • • • • • • • • • • • • • • • • • • • • • • • • • •

### Prayer exercise: **Holding cross**

This exercise uses a carved wooden cross called a 'holding cross'. You can buy crosses like these – designed to be held comfortably in the palm of your hand – at most Christian bookshops. Failing that, tie two twigs together with string to make your own rudimentary cross.

Sit comfortably. Hold the cross in your hand and close your eyes.

Focus your attention on the way your hand holds the cross and thank God that you are held in God's loving care.

Now shift your attention to a person or situation where you are aware of need or suffering.

Imagine that you are holding that person or place as you hold the cross in your hand – securely, gently, lovingly. Be aware that you hold this person or place in the presence of God.

Now imagine this person or situation being held in God's hands. Picture God's hands. What do they look like?

In the book of Isaiah God says: 'See! I have engraved you on the palms of my hands' (Isaiah 49:16).

Silently think about the needs of the person or place you have 'held' and your hopes for them – or speak these thoughts aloud to God.

You may like to use this prayer, inserting your own concerns where there are blanks:

Almighty God,
You hold us in your tender hands.
I hold _____ before you with love and concern
as I now hold this cross.
Hold_____ in your everlasting arms –
arms that the crucified Christ stretched wide
to embrace all people.
May your touch bring healing and forgiveness.
Amen.

• • • • • • • • • • • • • • • • • • • • • • • • • • • • • • • • • •

## Prayer exercise: **Praying the news**

This exercise involves watching the TV news and using its contents
as the basis for prayer. If you are able to watch alone – or your
companions don't mind their viewing being disturbed! – pray out loud
as you watch. Alternatively jot down things that strike you and pray
immediately after the broadcast. If you find the news overly
upsetting, focus on one item only – as suggested on page 49.

Watch the TV news. As you watch, think about how the people you see
on the screen are feeling and what their needs are. 'Step towards them'
with compassion. Talk to God about what you see and hear. Imagine you
are carrying these people and situations to Jesus, like the friends of the
paralyzed man. As you pray, allow yourself to mourn with those who
mourn and rejoice with those who rejoice. Try to be non-judgmental and
don't assume you know what is best for the people you are praying for.
Ask God to surround them with light and love.

# 8  *Binding and loosing*

In Chapter 7 we explored the type of prayer we call 'intercession' and in Chapter 4 we thought about 'asking' prayer. Both 'pleading' (interceding) and 'asking' are actions that demand a response and which carry an expectation of change. And so we come to the crunch question: 'Does prayer actually *do* anything?'

Does prayer bring about changes of events? Does God intervene in human lives and in the natural order of things in response to our prayers? If God does, how do we square that with our understanding of free will (surely by making Creation free, God has voluntarily tied his hands behind his back – the alternative would be a puppet universe where God moved us about like pieces on a chessboard)? If God is already at work in the world, fashioning events and working out his purposes, then why does he need us to pray?

Many Christians talk about 'answers to prayer' – interpreting improved circumstances as an indication that petitions and requests have been heard and acted upon. But what about prayers that seem to be unanswered? The ill friend who doesn't get better, the failed marriage that isn't repaired, the longed-for peace settlement that breaks down in chaos and disagreement? How do we make sense of these?

There are no easy answers to these questions. The Bible, however, sheds helpful light:

> *Do not be anxious about anything, but in everything, by prayer and petition, with thanksgiving, present your requests to God.*
> Philippians 4:6

The apostle Paul writing to the Philippian Christians urges them to bring the things that concern them to God in

prayer. If we have a relationship with God as our heavenly parent then communicating our worries and longings to God is a natural part of that relationship of trust. By praying, we develop and cement this relationship. We express our trust in God's goodness and his divine purposes.

In the Gospels, Jesus talks about prayer as an active thing, using the imagery of keys and locks, tying and untying, binding and loosing.

'The prayer of a righteous person is powerful and effective.'

James 5:16

> '*I will give you the keys of the kingdom; whatever you bind on earth will be bound in heaven, and whatever you loose on earth will be loosed in heaven.*'
> Matthew 16:19

This statement, addressed to the disciple Peter, suggests that Christ's followers are being entrusted as co-workers in the kingdom and that their prayers will carry some authority.

By praying, we become active participants in God's plans

— a very different image from pieces on a chessboard. As one American church's website puts it:

> [Prayer] is what can prise us from our seats as spectators and can make us active participants with God.

Let's think a little more about this idea of tying and untying. Jesus, in Luke's Gospel, announces the start of his earthly ministry with a bold manifesto:

> *'He has sent me to proclaim freedom for the prisoners and recovery of sight for the blind, to release the oppressed, to proclaim the year of the Lord's favour.'*
> Luke 4:18–19

Liberation, release, the untying of things that bind and oppress, loosing of 'chains' — all are at the heart of Jesus' purposes. The language Jesus uses here echoes passages from the Old Testament such as Isaiah 58:6, where God expresses his longing to see his people 'loose the chains of injustice and untie the cords of the yoke'.

As we pray — for healing, for reconciliation, for transformation in God's world — we co-operate with Jesus in his work of liberation. We aren't trying to change God's

mind about the world, we are *tuning in* to God's mind – dancing in step with God's desire to bring all Creation to wholeness and completion.

Perhaps our sense that prayers sometimes go 'unanswered' is linked to our inability to see God's purposes fully. We instinctively ask for a 'quick fix' – we want things to 'get better', to be smooth and painless, nice not nasty. Maybe sometimes God has deeper transformative desires that we are slow to see. I know from my own experience that when my life feels good and trouble-free I am more inclined to be superficial, complacent, less compassionate, less mindful of my need for God. So why do I unthinkingly ask for ease and well-being for others? Perhaps my prayers should be less about smoothing and soothing and more about delving and disturbing!

So what of the effectiveness of prayer? There is a wonderful – and darkly comic – story in the Acts of the Apostles (Acts 12:1–17). Peter has been imprisoned as part of King Herod's persecution of the first Christians and is being held by a squad of armed soldiers. The rest of the Christian believers are praying for him in secret. During the night, a miraculous event occurs in which an angel appears to Peter, the chains fall from his wrists and he is led to freedom past the oblivious guards. Peter goes immediately to the house where his fellow-believers are praying and knocks at the door. When a servant girl tells the believers that Peter is at the door they accuse her of seeing things – little thinking that their prayers have been answered and something unexpected and wonderful has occurred.

Prayer in this case *has* been effective – what they have been asking for and what has actually happened marvellously match up – yet they hardly dare to believe it.

Whether or not we understand the mechanics of what happens when we pray, we should pray anyway; pray in faith that it will somehow, perhaps in ways we'll never fully grasp, make a difference.

Prayer will certainly make a difference to the way we view the world – and in turn to how we act.

> **'This is the final test of effective prayer: does it make us burn with love, ache with compassion and thirst for justice? Does it open our eyes to a renewed vision for the world? Does it lift us up to heaven? Does it show us the kingdom? Does it set us on fire?'**
>
> *Stephen Cottrell*

• • • • • • • • • • • • • • • • • • • • • • • • • • • • • • • • • • • • • •

## Prayer exercise: **'Untying the yoke'**

This exercise takes the image of untying something that is bound in slavery as a symbol of God's liberating work in the world. It combines a physical action with prayer and silence.

You will need a ball of string or a length of washing line and an upright dining chair.

Start by making a list of situations or people about whom you are concerned. Focus your attention especially on ways in which these people or circumstances are messed up or bound and enslaved in some way. For example, someone you know may have debts or an addiction of some kind; another may be trapped in a destructive or abusive relationship; a community or country may be ensnared by greed or cycles of violence. A situation may seem intractable and hopeless – like a tangled ball of string full of knots.

Tie up a chair with string or rope. Wrap the string several times around the chair so that it is well bound. (If you are outside you could wrap string around the trunk of a tree instead.)

Now focus your attention on each of your concerns in turn and as you think about them, slowly unwind the string, collecting it into a ball. As you 'untie' the chair, speak to God in your own words about your concerns and your longing for him to bring liberation and wholeness – or simply do the untying in silence.

You may like to conclude with Jesus' words:

*'Whatever you loose on earth will be loosed in heaven.'*

• • • • • • • • • • • • • • • • • • • • • • • • • • • • • • • • • • • • •

## Prayer exercise: **Set your people free**

This exercise uses a framework of words to shape your prayers for the needs of the world. If you are doing this as a group, join together for the words in bold type. You might like to leave pauses between each section in order to pray silently or in your own words for specific people and places.

Liberating God, we pray for our world.
May your people care for the environment, respect each other
and live as you intended.
**Hear our prayer and set your people free.**

Merciful God, we pray for countries where there is war.
May hope and vision untangle the cords of hatred and division and
may those whose lives have been blighted by violence be
liberated from bitterness.
**Hear our prayer and set your people free.**

Compassionate God, we pray for those who live in poverty.
May they be set free from the bondage of other people's greed and
indifference and released from the chains of injustice and despair.
**Hear our prayer and set your people free.**

Life-giving God, we pray for those whose lives are dominated by
illness, disability or pain.
May they find comfort and relief and the liberation of loving care.
**Hear our prayer and set your people free.**

Powerful God, we pray for those in the grip of addiction or debt
and for those whose lives are spoilt by vicious circles of abuse
and neglect.
May the truth set them free and your healing untie the yoke of
their oppression.
**Hear our prayer and set your people free.**

Father God, we pray for all whose lives are ruled by fear and for
those whose minds are tied in knots with worry or depression.
May they know the freedom of peace that only you can bring.
**Hear our prayer and set your people free. Amen.**

# 9  *Teach us to pray*

**'Do you
wish to find
out the
really
sublime?
Repeat the
Lord's
Prayer.'**

*Napoleon
Bonaparte*

So far we've looked at eight different aspects of prayer: encounter, celebration, awareness, asking, listening, penitence, intercession, and binding and loosing. All these strands come together in the prayer we call the Lord's Prayer. This is the prayer Jesus taught his disciples in response to their question, 'How should we pray?' It might be more appropriately called 'the Disciple's Prayer' as it is a tool for learners – a template for all who are journeying in prayer. The Lord's Prayer is based on the words of Jesus as recorded in Luke 11:2–4 and Matthew 6:9–13.

> *Our Father in heaven,*
> *hallowed be your name,*
> *your kingdom come,*
> *your will be done,*
> *on earth as in heaven.*
> *Give us today our daily bread.*
> *Forgive us our sins*
> *as we forgive those who sin against us.*
> *Lead us not into temptation*
> *but deliver us from evil.*
> *For the kingdom, the power, and the glory are yours,*
> *now and for ever.*
> *Amen.*

Let's look at this prayer one phrase at a time.

## *'Our Father in heaven…'*

This prayer – like all prayer – starts with a relationship. The word Jesus uses is the intimate word 'Abba' – which means 'Daddy'. He calls God 'Abba' and he invites us to do the same when we pray.

### '...hallowed be your name...'

We give God praise and thanksgiving, fixing our gaze on God's holiness, beauty and tenderness. This celebrating and 'hallowing' of God is what we explored in Chapter 2. It is the way we focus our lens on God and acknowledge God's magnificence.

### '...your kingdom come, your will be done, on earth as in heaven...'

Here we acknowledge that God's plan for the world and for our lives surpasses ours. We bring our yearning for things to be as God intends – lamenting the ways in which the world is 'out of kilter' (Chapter 6), and praying that God's healing and wholeness may come (Chapters 7 and 8). We also commit ourselves to listening to God (Chapter 5) in order to discern God's priorities.

### '*Give us today our daily bread...*'

This is the 'asking' prayer we considered in Chapter 4. Having focused on the big picture (God's kingdom coming on earth) we turn our attention to our own needs – asking that we will have the things we really need (which isn't necessarily the same as the things we *want*). Because this is a communal prayer shared by Christians throughout the world, we pray these words alongside those whose basic needs may be more urgent and pressing than ours. This phrase calls us to assess our own lifestyle and priorities and respond to the needs of those who lack food, water and shelter.

### '*Forgive us our sins, as we forgive those who sin against us...*'

Asking God's forgiveness for the wrong things we do – or penitence (Chapter 6) – follows on from an awareness of our own need. We recognize our responsibility to pass on the forgiveness we receive, forgiving those who wrong or hurt us.

### '*Lead us not into temptation but deliver us from evil...*'

Living with an awareness of God's presence (Chapter 3) also brings an awareness of the evil forces that oppose God's reign of love. Jesus advises us to pray for the strength to resist all that is evil and to choose life not death.

### '*For the kingdom, the power, and the glory are yours, now and for ever...*'

Despite the brokenness of the world, the evil which spoils it and our own feeble mistakes, God is sovereign and is working out his purposes. We acknowledge this in a statement of faith. God is good and his love endures forever. Just as we called him Father, now we call him Lord.

Because the Lord's Prayer is so familiar it can be helpful to view it in a fresh light by reinterpreting it. Here are three versions of Jesus' prayer:

### Text Message Lord's Prayer
God@heaven.org. You rule, up and down.
We need grub and a break.
Will pass it on. Keep us focused.
You totally rule, long term.
Amen.

SHIP OF FOOLS WEBSITE

### The prayer of Jesus (Lord's Prayer)
God, who cares for us,
The wonder of whose presence fills us with awe.
Let kindness, justice and love shine in our world.
Let your secrets be known here as they are in
    heaven.
Give us the food and the hope we need for today.
Forgive us our wrongdoing
As we forgive the wrongs done to us.
Protect us from pride and from despair
And from the fear and hate that can swallow us up.
In you is truth, meaning, glory and power,
While worlds come and go.
Amen.

MONICA FURLONG

### Lord's Prayer
God (Daddy): Respect!
We want more of God on earth, more of his
    influence.
What you want will be done, on earth like it is in
    heaven.
Please give us everything you think we need.
I'm willing to admit what I've done,
and I accept that if I'm unable to forgive others
then why should I deserve to receive forgiveness?

Don't let us be tempted, and keep us away from
   horrible things.
The kingdom of heaven is yours,
you have power over absolutely everything and you
   are hugely glorified,
that is, 'you the man', for ever and ever.
Amen.

'LIVING ROOM' YOUTH GROUP, CHRIST CHURCH, CHELTENHAM

## Prayer exercise: **One phrase at a time...**

*A naval officer was once praying the Lord's Prayer with a friend in a
remote corner of Iceland. 'Say it slowly,' he said. 'Each phrase weighs
a ton.'*

John Pritchard

This exercise invites you to pray the Lord's Prayer very slowly and to
'chew' each phrase for its full meaning. You could do this during the
course of a day, or take one line a day for seven days, or even one

line a week over a number of weeks. Stay with each phrase for as long as you want to, using it as a springboard for your own thoughts and prayers. For each section of the prayer I have suggested ideas you might like to 'bounce' into.

### Our Father in heaven…

Think: What does it mean to call God 'father'? What is my picture of God? How is God like or unlike my human father? Is God my mother also?

### …hallowed be your name…

*Think:* How can I 'hallow' God in my daily life today? What does it mean to call God 'holy'? Do I acknowledge God's holiness in the way I live?

### …your kingdom come, your will be done, on earth as in heaven.

*Think:* What are God's desires and priorities for our world? What is God's kingdom like? (Many of Jesus' parables in the Gospels answer this question in picture language, for example, Matthew 20:1–16, Luke 15:3–10, Luke 15:11–32) What actions does God want me to take to help bring in the kingdom? Are there things about the way I spend my time and my money that obstruct the coming of the kingdom on earth?

### Give us today our daily bread.

*Think:* What are the things I really need? How much do I depend on God's provision and goodness? How can I meet the needs of others who have less than I do?

### Forgive us our sins as we forgive those who sin against us.

*Think:* What have I done, said or thought – or not done, said or thought – that has wounded others and angered God? Are there grudges and resentments I harbour against someone who has hurt me? Are there areas of my life where I need to face up to my mistakes?

### Lead us not into temptation but deliver us from evil.

*Think:* What are the things that are evil in God's sight? What are the things that distort my thinking and pull me away from following Jesus?

What are some of the things I should oppose and seek to change? How can we engage with the society we live in without being pulled out of shape by it?

**For the kingdom, the power, and the glory are yours, now and for ever. Amen**

*Think:* Do I really believe God is in control of things? Where in my life do I experience God's power? And where do I glimpse God's glory?

● ● ● ● ● ● ● ● ● ● ● ● ● ● ● ● ● ● ● ● ● ● ● ● ● ● ● ● ● ● ● ● ● ● ● ● ● ● ● ●

## Prayer exercise: Write your own version

This exercise encourages you to put Jesus' prayer into your own words and make it your own.

Read the Lord's Prayer, spending time thinking about the meaning of each phrase. Have a go at writing your own version. If you are doing this in a group share your prayers with each other.

# PART TWO

# How to pray

# 10  *Praying alone*

Sometimes when we pray, we will be in the company of other people. For example, if we attend a church, we will pray as part of a service, or we may get together with like-minded friends. Often, however, we will be alone – by ourselves with God – and it is on this personal, individual form of prayer that this chapter focuses.

It's worth noting that *whenever* we pray – whether with others or alone – we mingle our prayers with those of praying people who have lived and died before us (whom Christians call 'the Saints'), and share in the prayers of believers throughout the globe. In this sense our prayers, though they may be personal, are never private.

Jesus, teaching about prayer in what is often called 'the Sermon on the Mount', advised his listeners to pray discreetly and by themselves. He said:

> '...whenever you pray, go into your room and shut the door and pray to your Father who is in secret. And your Father who sees in secret will reward you.'
> Matthew 6:6

In the Gospels, Jesus models this intimate, personal style of prayer himself. He often withdraws from the company of others to a desert place, a mountain or an isolated lake to be alone with God.

So how can we imitate Jesus in this practice of quiet, secret prayer? How can we find rhythms of prayer in our daily lives that work for us and nourish our relationship with God? How can we find spaces to meet with God?

Some people have special places where they go to pray. You might like to find a special 'holy' place of your own. This could be a quiet church near your workplace that you can slip into during your lunch hour. It could be the cloisters of a city cathedral – a place with a sense of history where prayers have been said for generations.

But your special place could equally be a particular chair or corner in your house. It could be a hill you like to walk on or a favourite bench in a local park or a view from your window.

If no actual known place comes to mind you could create an imaginary place where you can go to be with God. You could, for example, visualize an 'island' of prayer – imagining the causeway that will lead you there, the ring of water that will temporarily seal you off from the cares and activities of the day, the special spot where you will sit to meet with God, and then the journey back across the causeway to resume 'real life' connections.

Spending a period of time quietly with God each day – wherever you choose to do it – is a good pattern to develop. This may be first thing in the morning or, if you aren't a 'mornings person', it may be at midday, or when you get

home from work, or last thing at night. Try to find a rhythm of prayer that works for you and fits with your lifestyle and personality type. Experiment a bit and see what suits you best, and don't be too hard on yourself if you find something doesn't work.

In some phases of life it may be very difficult to find a regular time to pray each day. If you have small children, or are caring for an elderly or ill relative, or have a very demanding job, you may find it impossible to carve out even ten minutes of 'quiet time' on a daily basis.

For you, finding time to pray may perhaps be a matter of identifying a block of time you already spend on something else and weaving prayer in and among it. For example, you could pray while in the shower each morning. You could pray as you walk your dog or wash up the breakfast dishes or drive to work. Your 'holy place' might in fact be your sink, your work desk or your shower cubicle!

Weaving prayer into the day-to-day tasks of our lives is not only practical; it is also profound, because it underlines for us the wholeness of our lives — that God is in the 'ordinary' making it extraordinary, that there is no division of spiritual and 'non-spiritual', that God is *in all things* and heaven and earth are tied together.

**'Find God in all things.'**

*Ignatius Loyola*

Think about the rhythms and routines of your life and see if you can identify parts of the week when you could pray. There might be a particular car journey you make, a time when you garden or do the ironing, or a slot when you exercise. You might find you can pray while swimming or weeding or feeding the baby or lying in the bath.

Perhaps if you travel by train or bus you could carry a small cross in your pocket (or a pebble) to remind you of God's presence or to bring to mind a particular person or situation you want to carry to God in prayer.

This mingling of tasks and prayer is what we might call 'in-and-among prayer'. Like everything it takes practice, so experiment a little. The following prayer exercises are designed to help you explore ways of praying in your daily life. Use these as a starting point for your own ideas in order to find patterns that work for you. A seventeenth-century French monk called Brother Lawrence – himself a bit of an expert in integrating prayer into domestic life – wrote this:

> The time of action does not differ from that time of prayer. I possess God as peacefully in the bustle of my kitchen… as I do upon my knees before the blessed sacrament… I turn my little omelette in the pan for the love of God. When it is finished, if I have nothing to do, I prostrate myself on the ground and worship my God, who gave me this grace to make it, after which I arise happier than a king.
>
> BROTHER LAWRENCE

• • • • • • • • • • • • • • • • • • • • • • • • • • • • • • • • • •

## Prayer exercise: Swimming the fruits of the Spirit

This prayer exercise is designed to be done while swimming lengths but you could do it with other rhythmic activities such as walking, mowing, knitting or ironing. Choose an activity that doesn't require your full concentration and where you are in no danger if your mind drifts onto another 'plane'.

The exercise takes, as its framework, the list of qualities that the apostle Paul calls the 'fruits of the Spirit' in Galatians 5:22 – *love, joy, peace, patience, kindness, goodness, gentleness, faithfulness and self-control*. You might want to try and memorize this list before you take to the water!

You could use this for personal reflective prayer – praying for yourself – or as a method of praying for someone else. I have sometimes used this exercise to pray for my three godchildren, focusing for one length on each 'fruit' for each godchild in turn – which requires me to swim at least twenty-seven lengths of the pool! I find the discipline of spending one length on each quality keeps my grasshopper brain from bouncing off into other thoughts too much.

Start by repeating the word **love** in your mind as you swim. Synchronize the repetition of the word with your strokes. Now think of the person you are praying for. Thank God for them – for the love you have for them, for the love others show them and for the love they give to others. Pray that they may grow in love, be loving towards others, be blessed by love that is unconditional and life-giving, and become ever more aware of how much God loves them.

Now move on to **joy** (do this as you change direction, or begin a new row of knitting or begin another section of your walk). Again, focus on the person you are praying for. If they are especially joyful, thank God for this. If they are short of joy ask God to fill them with the bubbling, abundant joy that God's Spirit can give. Imagine what that person will look and sound like with this joy welling up in them and hold this mental image before God. If there are particular reasons why this person is without joy carry these circumstances and concerns to God.

Continue with **peace** – asking God to give this person his peace, praying for issues that make the person anxious and take away peace of mind, carrying to God any situations of conflict or unrest.

Do the same with **patience, kindness, goodness, gentleness, faithfulness** and **self-control**. Spend time on each quality, repeating the word in your mind in time with your movements, thanking God for all he is doing already and asking him to bless the person you are praying for with this particular quality. Use each of the nine 'fruits' as springboards into other thoughts and prayers.

● ● ● ● ● ● ● ● ● ● ● ● ● ● ● ● ● ● ● ● ● ● ● ● ● ● ● ● ● ● ● ● ● ● ● ● ● ● ● ● ● ● ● ●

## Prayer exercise: **Five-finger prayers**

If you lack confidence when praying alone in your own words, this exercise will give you a simple structure to focus your prayers. It uses the five fingers of one hand to help you remember a five-part structure. You could do it while waiting for a bus, waiting for a kettle to boil or in a quiet ten minutes at the beginning or end of the day. Spend as long with each 'finger' as you want to.

Start with one of your fists clenched. Uncurl the fingers one at a time in this order:

**Thumb**   Thumb prayers are about the 'thumbs up' gesture – the things that are good. Spend time thanking God in your own words for all that is good about your life or the lives of those you care about.

**Index finger**   This is the finger that normally points. Turn your prayers to direction and guidance. What decisions are you currently involved in making? Where do you or others need wisdom and discernment or fresh ideas? Are there areas of life where hard choices have to be made? Bring these concerns to God.

**Middle finger**   The middle finger is the biggest. Turn your attention now to praying for the powerful – governments, business directors, politicians, community leaders. Ask God to 'let his kingdom come'. Pray for wisdom, justice, peace and kindness. As you pray, ask God what his priorities are and where he wants you to take action to make a difference.

**Ring finger**   Now pray for those you love. Voice particular concerns to God.

**Little finger**   This finger is the weakest. It reminds us to pray for the vulnerable – people you know who are sick, depressed, lonely, bereaved, homeless.

Now that your hand is fully open, lay it palm upwards in your lap. Finish by asking that – just as your hand is open – you may be open to God and to the needs of others for the remainder of the day.

# 11 Praying with others

As well as praying on our own it can be good to pray with other people. Community is central to many faiths. In Christianity, believers are collectively described as 'the body of Christ'. Inter-dependence, shared lives and mutual care are important elements of growing in faith together. In the days of the early church – a time excitingly described in the Acts of the Apostles – Christians were committed to meeting together in each other's homes.

This communal sense of solidarity and shared faith was at the heart of the new-born church as it grew and spread.

Jesus encourages his followers to meet together in prayer, saying:

> 'For where two or three are gathered in my name, I am
> there among them.'
> Matthew 18:20

The promise of Jesus is that when people meet with each other he will also meet with them.

In the Old Testament, God promises that if his people are of one mind in their praying – coming before him, humbly, with a shared agenda – then he will act and bring healing.

> '. . .if my people who are called by my name humble
> themselves, and pray and seek my face and turn from
> their wicked ways, then I will hear from heaven, and will
> forgive their sin and heal their land.'
> 2 Chronicles 7:14

Christians meet together to share their prayers with one another when they attend 'services' (acts of corporate worship). In addition to this, many like to meet in small groups – as 'prayer partners' or in 'prayer triplets' – or in groups sometimes called

'They spent their time learning from the apostles, and they were like family to each other. They also broke bread and prayed together.'

*Acts 2:42*

'home groups' or 'cell groups'. Sharing concerns and joining others in prayer can be a great source of support and mutual encouragement, strengthening the sense of belonging together.

Praying together in this way may involve words spoken out loud (either improvised 'extemporary' prayers or written 'liturgical' prayers) but it may also involve praying silently together.

You may feel more comfortable with one style of corporate prayer than with another. Praying out loud with others can seem a little intimidating but there is great value in hearing one another's prayers. If you are uncertain about praying in this way you could write prayers down and read them aloud until you begin to feel more at home with it.

If you have no one you could meet with in this way, remember that when any one person prays, they share in the prayers of Christians everywhere and across all generations.

The following exercises are designed to be done by groups of four or more people.

• • • • • • • • • • • • • • • • • • • • • • • • • • • • • • • • • •

## Prayer exercise: **Strands of wool**

This exercise gives a framework for a group of people praying together. It is particularly useful if extemporary (improvised) prayer is an unfamiliar activity for group members as it gets people talking and moving about very naturally.

You will need several strands of coloured wool (the more colours the better) – enough for three strands per person. Cut the wool into 6-inch (15-cm) lengths and give three strands of differing colours to each person (you could knot them loosely in threes to make this easier).

Give each person three strands of wool.

Invite people to swap *one* strand with someone else and to exchange ideas of *one thing to give thanks to God for*. Remaining in these pairs, pray together either aloud or silently.

Now invite people to swap another strand with someone else and identify *one situation or issue that concerns them* – either personal or global. Pray as before.

> 'Within the body of the Church we are supported and encouraged by each other's prayers. At any one time when you sit down to say your prayers there are countless millions of Christian people all around the world who are also praying. You probably cannot hear them; you may feel very isolated in your own faith, perhaps because it is not shared by your family and your friends, but the truth remains: you are not alone.'
>
> *Stephen Cottrell*

Now swap the third strand with someone different and exchange ideas about *one person you are concerned for*. (You might want to keep the person's name to yourself to protect their confidentiality.) Pray together – carrying this person to Jesus.

When you have prayed (silently or out loud) with three other people – and acquired three new strands of wool – knot the three strands end-to-end to make one long strand. Stand in a circle and tie the end of your wool to the end of that of the person next to you so that you create a continuous chain of wool. Holding this 'chain of prayer' as a sign of your unity and connectedness you could conclude your prayers by saying this prayer (which is often called 'The Grace'):

> May the grace of our Lord Jesus Christ
> and the love of God
> and the fellowship of the Holy Spirit
> be with us all, ever more.
> Amen.

• • • • • • • • • • • • • • • • • • • • • • • • • • • • • • • • • • • • •

## Prayer exercise: **'For all the sick ones'**

This exercise gives you the opportunity to use a liturgy, or written form of prayer. These words have been carefully crafted so that there is a sense of music and rhythm to them and they are – to some extent – like poetry. We don't of course need to use special 'poetic' language to address God, but sometimes using creative liturgies can give fresh insights as we pray and help us to avoid language that has become clichéd or 'tired'.

This liturgy by the writer Nicola Slee is an original way of praying for the needs of others – and our own needs. You could take turns to say a three-line stanza and then join together on the word 'mercy'. Alternatively have one person say the verses and simply say 'mercy' collectively.

| | |
|---|---|
| For all the sick ones | |
| For all the stuck ones | |
| For all the down-on-their-luck ones | mercy |
| | |
| For the paralyzed | |
| For the terrified | |
| For the mortified | mercy |
| | |
| For those who can't finish | |
| For those who won't fulfil their promise | |
| For the ones who never got started | mercy |
| | |
| For the ones stuck in their cells | |
| For the ones stuck in their beds | |
| For the ones stuck in their heads | mercy |
| | |
| For all the ravers | |
| For all the mourners | |
| For all the demented | mercy |
| | |
| For the bleeding | |
| For the pleading | |
| For the unheeding | mercy |
| | |
| For our lack of madness | |
| For our unfeeling sadness | |
| For our soul's paralysis | mercy |
| | |
| For all the sick ones | |

# 12   *Praying with our senses*

As a child I was encouraged to pray with my hands together and my eyes closed, presumably so that I didn't fidget and get distracted. It's only as an adult that I've learnt to pray with my eyes open and to use my senses in my prayers.

We come to God as whole people – not just as brains on legs!

The Old Testament commands us to love God with every part of our selves:

> *You shall love the Lord your God with all your heart and with all your soul and with all your might.*
> Deuteronomy 6:5

Our whole selves include our sense of sight, hearing, smell, taste and touch. We can love God and communicate with God through our senses. God can love us and communicate with us through our senses too. The next few chapters will focus on ways in which we can explore our senses in prayer.

'There is a road from the eye to the heart that does not go through the intellect.'

*G. K. Chesterton*

## *Sense of sight*

Visual perception can enhance our awareness of God – in the beauty of Creation, in the contemplation of a particular picture or object, in the expressions on other people's faces. Many people like to pray looking at a candle flame or at an icon. We will look more closely at using pictures in prayer in Chapter 13 and at making our own pictures and objects as we pray in Chapter 20.

## *Sense of hearing*

Sound is important as we pray, as indeed is silence. Many people associate prayer with words – we speak of 'saying our prayers'. (One contemporary comedian unsympathetically described Christian practice as 'mumbling in cold buildings'!) But music and song are important in prayer too. Music can touch us at a deep level and connect with buried memories and emotions. If we are coming to God with our *whole selves* then these unconscious parts of ourselves are important too. Chapter 14 will focus on music in prayer.

## *Senses of smell and taste*

Our senses of smell and taste can be part of our prayer life too. Many Christian traditions – and indeed Jewish practice – use incense as part of corporate worship. Its strong fragrance symbolizes prayer itself, filling the air and rising to God as an offering. Chapter 15 will explore taste and smell more fully and suggest some ways of using these senses creatively.

## *Sense of touch*

Chapter 16 will consider our sense of touch in prayer. Tactile praying is something that I became increasingly aware of through working with children, and particularly when my own children were small. We attended a Lent workshop once, where we were presented with a basket of materials and asked to put our hand inside and choose the thing that 'felt like God'. The basket included fur, felt, suede, ribbon, glittery sparkly fabric, foil, raffia, tinsel, and strings of beads. Identifying how my relationship with God felt at that particular moment was profoundly moving. As adults we often neglect touch – perhaps because as children we were told, *'Don't touch!'* Touching things that are hard or soft, cold or warm, smooth or rough helps us to make sense of more abstract things that might also feel 'rough' or 'cold' or 'hard'.

Praying in a multi-sensory way can add new dimensions to our prayer life and give us glimpses into deep truths. I was once part of an Easter service called 'Sensing the Passion' during the course of which images of Jesus on the cross were projected onto a screen while we listened to a mournful violin melody. We tasted honey (the sweetness of God's love) and vinegar (the 'sour wine' Jesus was offered during the crucifixion), smelt and handled myrrh (the aromatic oil with which Jesus' body was anointed after his  death), and touched barbed wire and sheep's wool (symbols of the pain and comfort of the cross). All five senses were engaged during the course of the service and these sensory experiences conveyed things to me that went beyond words.

The following prayer exercises are designed to help you get more in touch with your senses and to think about ways you can pray with your whole self.

• • • • • • • • • • • • • • • • • • • • • • • • • • • • • • • • • • • • •

## Prayer exercise: **God be in my head**

This prayer, known as the Sarum Primer, is a wonderful meditation on the desire for God to be in all parts of life – and indeed in death too. You might want to try and learn it by heart.

There is a lovely sung version of it, dating from the sixteenth century, which you'll find in *Hymns Ancient and Modern* or *Common Praise*.

Sit or stand in a relaxed but attentive posture.

Say (or sing) each line of the prayer slowly, leaving space for your thoughts and for the implications of each line to sink in.

You could touch your head, your eyes, your mouth and your heart as you focus on these parts of you. If you prefer to pray with your eyes closed then open them for the second line of the prayer and allow time for them to take in all you can see.

> God be in my head, and in my understanding;
> God be in my eyes, and in my looking;
> God be in my mouth, and in my speaking;
> God be in my heart, and in my thinking;
> God be at my end, and at my departing.

●●●●●●●●●●●●●●●●●●●●●●●●●●●●●●●●●●●●●●●●●

## Prayer exercise: Sensing God

Sit comfortably.

Think, in turn, of:

- Your favourite colour
- Your favourite sound
- Your favourite smell
- Your favourite taste
- Your favourite physical sensation

Thank God for all these things.

Now spend time thinking:

- What colour is God?
- What does God sound like?
- What does God smell like?
- What does God taste like?
- What does God feel like?

'My soul
can find no
staircase to
heaven
unless it be
through
earth's
loveliness.'

*Michelangelo*

Let your imagination explore these ideas. Invite God to reveal himself to you as you ponder.

You could conclude with the following prayer:

> God of rainbows, we look for you.
> God of waterfalls and whispers, we listen for you.
> God of fragrance, we sense your presence.
> God of salt and sweetness, we taste you and know that
>     you are good.
> God of strength and tenderness, touch our lives.
> Amen.

# 13  *Praying with pictures*

In the last chapter we prayed: *'God be in my eyes, and in my looking...'* Here we explore how we can use our eyes in prayer and, specifically, how we can use pictures.

The question of how we can worship someone we cannot see has taxed many people down the centuries. How is it possible to imagine and know a God our eyes cannot perceive?

The apostle Paul, in the letter to the Colossians, describes Jesus as 'the image of the invisible God' (Colossians 1:15). Jesus, says Paul, is like a picture showing us what God is like.

Jesus himself provides many 'images' of God – as a shepherd, a vineyard owner, the father of a wayward son, a woman in search of something lost. The Old Testament describes God as a rock, a tower, a shelter, a hen gathering chicks, a lover wooing his beloved. All these 'pictures' contribute to our understanding of God's character and purposes.

But what is God's face like? Does God even have a face?

The Psalms talk of seeking God's face:

*My heart says of you, 'Seek his face!'*
*Your face, Lord, I will seek.*
Psalm 27:8

The book of Numbers in the Old Testament describes God turning his face towards us, as a sign of blessing. The priest Aaron is told to bless the people with these words:

*'The Lord make his face shine upon you*
*and be gracious to you;*
*the Lord turn his face toward you and give you peace.'*
Numbers 6:25–26

This idea that God's face is, in some way, shiny and luminous also appears in the book of Exodus – the book that describes the liberation of the people of Israel from slavery in Egypt by the prophet Moses (Aaron's brother). When Moses comes back from Mount Sinai where he has spoken with God, Moses' face is so radiant that others cannot bear to look at him. Having encountered God and spent time in his presence, Moses now mirrors God's brightness and glory.

> **'The eye**
> **with which**
> **I see God is**
> **the same**
> **eye with**
> **which God**
> **sees me.'**
>
> *Meister Eckhart*

*When Aaron and all the Israelites saw Moses, his face*
*was radiant, and they were afraid to come near him.*
Exodus 34:30

Psalm 34 picks up this idea of reflected radiance for the person who spends time in God's company.

*Those who look to him [God] are radiant; their faces are*
*never covered with shame.*
Psalm 34:5

Are we like Moses in this respect? Can other people tell from the look on our faces when we have spent time in prayer? Do we glow with holy tenderness when we have gazed at God? You may know of people for whom this is the case – people whose eyes shine with compassion and joy when they have been with God.

Contemplation – the word often used for the kind of 'practising the presence' praying that we explored in Chapter 3 – literally means 'gazing'. We gaze in love at God and God gazes in love at us. The writer of the Psalms says that there is nothing he wants to do more than gaze at God's loveliness.

> *One thing I ask of the Lord, this is what I seek:*
> *that I may dwell in the house of the Lord*
> *all the days of my life,*
> *to gaze upon the beauty of the Lord*
> *and to seek him in his temple.*
> Psalm 27:4

So how can we gaze at God? How can we see God's face?

In many parts of the Christian church – especially in the Eastern Orthodox tradition – icons are used in worship. These are painted images of Christ, his mother Mary, or particular saints. They are designed to be looked 'through' rather than 'at' – as windows which lead us to deeper understanding. They often incorporate symbols that draw attention to theological truths. For example, large eyes symbolize our 'spiritual eyes' that see beyond the material and surface things; large ears emphasize our willingness to listen to God's word; large heads draw attention to the importance of contemplation and prayer in spiritual growth. Colours are also used symbolically: blue reveals heaven and mystery; red is the colour of blood; gold represents the colour of God's glory and sanctity.

During the Reformation in sixteenth- and seventeenth-century Europe there were many arguments about religious pictures. Protestants believed that, since no image could adequately portray both the divinity and the humanity of Christ, then *any* visual image was blasphemous. They also believed that using pictures in worship encouraged people to be idolatrous and to worship the pictures themselves rather than the invisible God. As a consequence there was

'The real
voyage of
discovery
consists not
in seeking
new
landscapes,
but in
having new
eyes.'

*Marcel Proust*

widespread destruction of pictures, frescos and statues – 'iconoclasm' – and a mistrust of the senses in prayer and worship. We are still living with the legacy of this mistrust in some parts of the church but many other Christians are reclaiming the visual dimension in worship.

God is invisible and unfathomable, so no picture can ever do justice to God's nature or represent all aspects of God's personality. But pictures can 'speak' to us and illuminate particular qualities of God's divinity. The prayer exercise 'Mother and child' will help you, for example, to explore the motherhood and gentleness of God and to respond to God as a nurturing parent.

A second way that we can see God is in one another. If – as Christians believe – all humans are made in God's image, then all of our faces bear *some* resemblance to God's, in spite of the many things that mar and interfere with that divine likeness. When we look with tenderness, with pity, with empathy at one another then we see glimpses of the nature of God in one another's eyes. This 'eye contact' can help us both to pray and to perceive God.

The second prayer exercise 'Eyes open' helps us explore the way we can use the faces of others to guide our prayers.

• • • • • • • • • • • • • • • • • • • • • • • • • • • • • • • • • • • •

## Prayer exercise: **Mother and child**

The prophet Isaiah compares God's love to that of a mother. The passionate devotion of a mother for her child is the template for our understanding of God's involvement with us. God is *even more* committed to us than a human mother who suckles her baby at her breast.

> 'Can a mother forget the baby at her breast
> and have no compassion on the child she has borne?
> Though she may forget, I will not forget you!'
> Isaiah 49:15

Psalm 131 describes a soul at prayer as a contented child resting in its mother's arms.

...I have stilled and quietened my soul;
like a weaned child with its mother,
like a weaned child is my soul within me.

Psalm 131:2

**This prayer exercise provides an
opportunity for us to focus on God as a
mother and to use an icon – in this case a
depiction of Mary with the infant Christ –
as a window into mother–child love, and
in particular, God's mothering of us.**

Look firstly at the face of the mother, and
especially at her eyes. What emotions does
her face convey? Imagine that she is looking
at you. What does she say to you?

Now look at the way that she is
holding the child. What are her hands like?
Imagine that God is holding you in the way
she is holding the infant Jesus. Imagine that
you are close enough to sense the mother's
heartbeat, to feel her breath, to smell her
skin and hair.

Focus now on the child. How is he
feeling? Notice his hand touching his mother's clothes. Imagine that
contact, and the comfort and security it gives. Imagine that you are that
child with your cheek against your mother's cheek, responding to the joy
of being held.

Spend some time thinking about the ways in which God is like a
mother to you. This may stir up thoughts or memories about your own
mother or – if you are a mother – your relationship with your children.
Some of these thoughts may be good; others may be ambivalent or raw.
Whatever emotions surface, offer them to God in prayer.

You might like to conclude with this prayer:

Mothering God,
who gave us life,
brought us to birth in Christ
and welcomed us as your children,

shelter us in your arms,
feed us with your presence
and nurture your tender love in us.
Amen.

• • • • • • • • • • • • • • • • • • • • • • • • • • • • • • • • • • • • •

## Prayer exercise: **Eyes open**

This exercise invites you to take a news photograph and look closely at it – using the 'gate' of your eyes to stimulate prayer for the needs of others. You might like to collect photographs from the newspaper in advance so that you have a selection of images to choose from. (Choose people-centred stories that convey strong emotions – either positive or negative.)

Select a photograph and look closely at it.

What is going on in the picture and what are the issues that this piece of journalism raises?

Focus on the people in the picture – or on one person in particular.

What do you think this person is feeling?
What does he or she need?
What does he or she long for?
What do you think God might want to say to this person?

Spend some time 'holding' this person and his or her needs before God – either silently or using words spoken aloud.

If you are praying with others you might like to conclude with this blessing by the writer David Adam:

May you see Christ in others,
Be Christ to others,
That we may dwell in him, and he in us.

# 14 Praying with music

The last chapter explored 'praying with our eyes'. This one focuses on 'praying with our ears'.

Music is a powerful language. As a report into church music in the 1990s said:

> ...music... is one of the most accessible and universal languages, being less limited than speech by social, intellectual, national or religious boundaries. It expresses, often more effectively than words, our feelings and aspirations.
>
> IN TUNE WITH HEAVEN: THE REPORT OF THE ARCHBISHOPS'
> COMMISSION ON CHURCH MUSIC

'Where words fail, music speaks.'

*Hans Christian Andersen*

We can use music as we pray. We can listen to music made by other people and we can make it for ourselves.

Because music affects our mood and our emotions, listening to it can help to take us into a deep encounter with God. Depending on the music – and our response to it – it can disturb us, stir us up, free our thoughts, provoke longing, or fill us with peace and a sense of well-being. Music can lead us into the kind of thanksgiving prayer we discussed in Chapter 2; articulate the lamentation and penitence we explored in Chapter 6; and help us to listen to God in the ways we considered in Chapter 5. It can help us, both literally and metaphorically, to – as the poet John Milton wrote – 'keep in tune with heaven'.

But what about making our own music? Singing is often mentioned in the Bible. We are encouraged to sing to God and to 'sing a new song'.

'I will sing to the Lord,
for he is highly exalted.'
Exodus 15:1

*Sing to the Lord, all the earth...*
I Chronicles 16:23

*Sing to him a new song; play skilfully, and shout for joy.*
Psalm 33:3

*For you make me glad by your deeds, O Lord; I sing for joy at the work of your hands.*
Psalm 92:4

Singing is described as an expression of our joy and praise to God – an outpouring of our love and gratitude. According to the Psalms, even the trees sing to God!

*Then all the trees of the forest will sing for joy; they will sing before the Lord, for he comes...*
Psalm 96:12–13

The apostle Paul tells the Christians of the early church to sing.

*Sing and make music in your heart to the Lord.*
Ephesians 5:19

What does it mean to make music in our hearts for God? What is it about music that is so special? And what if we can't sing? (Or think we can't!)

Perhaps the value of singing is something to do with spontaneity. Artist Georgia O'Keefe said this:

> Singing has always seemed to me the most perfect means of expression. It is so spontaneous. And after singing, I think the violin. Since I cannot sing, I paint.

American gospel singer Mahalia Jackson – an inspirational figure in the Civil Rights movement who sang in Washington in 1963 just before Martin Luther King Jr delivered his 'I have a dream' speech – believed in the power of both song and prayer. Her words express this eloquently:

> When you sing gospel you have a feeling there is a cure for what's wrong... Blues are the songs of despair, but gospel songs are the songs of hope... I hope to bring people to God with my songs... Without a song, each day would be a century... Faith and prayer are the vitamins of the soul; man cannot live in health without them.

The following prayer exercises give you the opportunity to 'pray with your ears' and to sing to God – no matter how un-musical you may think you are.

'After silence, that which comes nearest to expressing the inexpressible is music...'

*Aldous Huxley*

• • • • • • • • • • • • • • • • • • • • • • • • • • • • • • • • • • • •

## Prayer exercise: **Listen!**

This exercise invites you to listen to a piece of music and use the ideas and feelings it stimulates as a form of prayer. Choose an instrumental piece of music in a style that you like that's about five

minutes long – preferably a piece that you find moving and beautiful. If you are short of ideas visit the music section in your local library or raid a friend's CD collection.

Sit comfortably or lie on the floor. Make sure you won't be disturbed and start the music.

Listen to the music with your eyes closed.

As you listen, let your mind wander but do this in the presence of God. Ask God to guide your thoughts.

If you find your thoughts wandering unduly into ideas that are banal, inappropriate or unhelpful, imagine that you are rounding them up again (sheepdog-like) and setting them back on track. Having captured your thoughts, focus again on the music and ask God to meet you in it.

You might like to conclude with this prayer:

God of sound and maker of music,
bringer of harmony and giver of joy,
hold our thoughts in your creative hands.

Resolve our discord, heal our broken rhythms
and help us to tune our hearts to your eternal song.
Amen.

## Prayer exercise: **Sing a new song**

This exercise is for you to do in secret with God so make sure (especially if you are self-conscious about singing) that you are in a place where no one will overhear you. Don't worry about the quality of your singing – God will be delighted by the outpourings of your words and feelings no matter what *you* think it sounds like!

Sit or stand in a private place. Offer your time to God, saying 'thank you' for the gift of music.

Now start to sing, either using a familiar tune or improvising a melody of your own. Start by singing without words – perhaps using a 'la' sound – then add the word 'Alleluia'.

Now make up whatever words you like to express your thoughts and feelings to God. Don't worry about the words rhyming or sounding polished. Fit them to your tune as best you can.

If you are able to play an instrument you might like to play along as well – improvising a simple beat or tune as you sing. Try not to think too hard – be spontaneous!

Use the music to say whatever you want to say to God.

You could conclude with these words that are sometimes known as the *Doxology*:

Praise God from whom all blessings flow,
Praise him all creatures here below.
Praise him above you heavenly host,
Praise Father, Son and Holy Ghost.

## 15 *Praying with taste and smell*

This chapter will explore our senses of taste and smell, both literally – as ways of enhancing our experience of prayer – and as metaphors for our encounters with God.

Psalm 34 says, 'Taste and see that the Lord is good...' We are being encouraged by the Psalmist to connect with God and to savour his presence with us, and this encounter is expressed in terms of eating and tasting. Another Psalm says this about God's words:

*How sweet are your words to my taste,*
*sweeter than honey to my mouth!*
Psalm 119:103

How then can the experience of eating and tasting heighten our understanding of God and God's love for us? Holy Communion – in which Christians eat bread and drink wine as symbols of Jesus' death – is one way of 'tasting' God's healing love. Literally eating and drinking basic staple commodities (bread and wine) underlines the everyday and 'earthed' core of Christian belief, bringing home to us that God is hiding in physical realities – in childbirth and death and all human experience.

The prayer exercise 'Bitter and sweet' is another idea for using taste as a part of prayer.

Fragrance is an important theme in the Old Testament. Over and over, the Jews are encouraged to burn offerings to God that will be a 'pleasing aroma before the Lord'. The burning of incense to create fragrance was both an essential part of Old Testament Jewish worship and a powerful symbol of the people's prayers. Psalm 141 likens prayer to incense:

*May my prayer be set before you like incense:*
*may the lifting up of my hands be like the evening*
  *sacrifice.*
Psalm 141:2

In the New Testament book of Revelation, prayer and incense are linked again. The apostle John describes the elders in heaven holding up golden bowls of incense 'which are the prayers of the saints' (Revelation 5:8).

Aromatherapists, who use aromatic oils from plants in massage treatment, operate on the understanding that smells can affect and enhance our mood and that certain fragrances lift our spirits and boost our sense of well-being. The book of Proverbs concurs with this, saying:

*Perfume and incense bring joy to the heart...*
Proverbs 27:9

Our sense of smell is closely linked to memory and to our emotional responses. Smelling an aroma we like can give us great pleasure. Perfume is part of the pleasure of the mutual love described in the book of the Bible known as the 'Song of Solomon' (or 'Song of Songs') – as indeed is taste. The Beloved's words about her Lover in this celebratory love poem are deeply sensuous:

*Let him kiss me with the kisses of his mouth –*
*For your love is more delightful than wine.*
*Pleasing is the fragrance of your perfumes:*
*Your name is like perfume poured out.*
Song of Songs 1:2–3

'Smell is a potent wizard that transports us across thousands of miles and all the years we have lived.'

*Helen Keller*

There is an incident in Jesus' life – described in the Gospels – when a woman comes to a house where Jesus is a guest, breaks open a jar of expensive perfume, and pours it on Jesus' head. One version of the story says that the house was filled with the fragrance of the perfume. Jesus welcomes the woman's action and the powerful symbolism of the fragrance. He turns to the critical onlookers and says, 'She has done a beautiful thing to me' (Mark 14:6).

How then can we incorporate the pleasure and symbolism of perfume and flavour into our prayer life? How can we encounter God through our taste buds and our sense of smell? And how can we use 'fragrance offerings' as symbols of the offering of our lives and our prayers to God?

How, too, can we *be* the 'fragrance of God' in the communities and families in which we live? Years ago there was an advert for Bisto in which two cartoon children were drawn towards a kitchen (where gravy was being made) by wafts of delicious aroma. Standing on tiptoe and sniffing with all their might they said, 'Ah… Bisto!' The challenge of the Christian life is to live in such a way that people around us catch the fragrance of God and respond as if saying, 'Ah… Jesus!'

You could try using fragrance as a way of marking out a special time for prayer, beginning by rubbing scented oil or balm on your hands or dabbing it on your forehead. Or you could light a scented candle or a burner with essential oils in it.

●●●●●●●●●●●●●●●●●●●●●●●●●●●●●●●●●●●●●●●

'Come and dine, the master calleth, come and dine. You may feast at Jesus' table all the time…'

*C. B. Widmeyer*

## Prayer exercise: **Bitter and sweet**

For this prayer you will need a slice of lemon and something sweet such as a piece of chocolate. The idea of the exercise is to focus attention in a heightened way on the things in our lives – and in the world – which are bitter and sweet, and to bring these things to God in prayer.

Sit comfortably and try to relax.

Taste the slice of lemon, becoming aware of the sourness of it and its effect on your lips and tongue.

Use this sensation of bitterness to 'carry your thoughts' to situations and circumstances that are harsh or bitter. These might be personal things such as a broken relationship, or an incidence of conflict, or more global things such as fighting or racial tension.

Bring these things – and your feelings about them – to God in your own words. Now spend a few moments thinking about Jesus suffering on the cross and the bitterness of rejection and hatred that he endured.

Now eat the piece of chocolate, enjoying its sweetness.

As you eat it think about God's love for you, for your community and for the world. Thank God for this sweet love and pray that you will be able to share it authentically with others.

Spend a few moments thinking about Jesus' resurrection and the transforming power of hope. Pray for this hope to make a difference in parts of the world where there is despair.

You could end your time of prayer with these words:

> Christ, who tasted the bitter cross and
> who shares our pain,
> be with all those who suffer
> and with those for whom life has turned sour.
> Lord, risen from the dead and full of glory,
> fill us with your sweet love.
> May we taste your goodness and share it with others.
> Amen.

## Prayer exercise: **Beautiful fragrance**

This exercise invites you to think about all that is good in your life and in the world using the stimulus of a smell you like to help you make connections. You will need to find something that you like the smell of, that you can hold or reach while praying. This will be different for everyone – especially as smells connect powerfully with our memories – but possibilities might include soap, a lemon, some herbs, a flower, coffee, essential oils, a creosoted fence, a baby's head!

Hold the aromatic thing or (if it isn't portable) sit or stand close enough to smell it easily.

Breathe in deeply and slowly, inhaling the smell and savouring it.

Spend a while just enjoying the fragrance and thanking God for it and for its associations.

Now think of all that is good in your life. This might include relationships, work, special places, memories, health, as well as material things such as food, water and shelter. You might like to name things out loud to God as you think of them, perhaps using a repeated phrase such as '_____ is good. Thank you, God.'

Continue breathing in the pleasant smell and now focus on all that is good about God. Again you could speak aloud saying, 'You are good because _____.'

Finally – continuing to sniff the fragrance – think of the good you would like to do in other people's lives. Ask God to help you do this.

You could end with this prayer of Cardinal John Neuman (the former archbishop of Philadelphia), which was a favourite prayer of Mother Teresa:

> *Dear Jesus, help me to spread Your fragrance everywhere I go. Penetrate and possess my whole being so utterly that all my life may only be a radiance of Yours. Shine through me and be so in me, that every soul I come in contact with may feel Your Presence in my soul: let them look up and see no longer me – but only You, my Jesus.*
>
> Cardinal John Neuman

# 16  *Praying with touch*

Chapter 12 looked at the power of the senses in communication and understanding – and therefore in prayer. This chapter focuses specifically on our sense of touch.

Jesus taught in a very down-to-earth way and his teaching often made reference to everyday objects or situations. He told stories about rock, sand, bread, yeast, pearls and seeds. I sometimes imagine that he may have picked these things up – held them, handled them, maybe even passed them round the crowd – as he was speaking. He knew the power of visual and tactile metaphors to make abstract spiritual truths comprehensible to earth-bound human minds.

Touch was important in Jesus' healing ministry too. He touched lepers, spread mud onto a blind man's eyes, and put his fingers into the ears of a deaf man as he healed him. Jesus' approach to people was very hands-on.

Touch is important to us – especially at times of life when we feel isolated or vulnerable. The organization PAT (Pets as Therapy) recognizes the value of touch for people who are ill, taking dogs and cats into hospitals and hospices so that patients can pet and stroke them. There is something enormously therapeutic about stroking fur. Animals curled up asleep give off a palpable sense of peace and well-being.

D. H. Lawrence, in his poem *Pax*, describes a person at one with the living God as being like a cat asleep on a chair in the master's house. If you have a cat or a dog – especially if you have one that will curl up and go to sleep on your lap or by your feet – you could spend some time quietly observing it as it rests, and imagine yourself curled on God's lap, at peace.

Many people like to pray while holding something. The

rosary is an obvious example of this, where a special string of beads is used as an aide to prayer. In Chapter 7 we explored the use of a holding cross. Holding pebbles can also be useful. For example, you could find two pebbles – one rough and one smooth – and use these to help you pray for things that are 'rough' and for things that are good. Simply hold them in your hands and let their texture and shape inform your prayers.

If you are praying for a situation that feels very heavy and burdensome you could hold a bigger stone in your hands – reflecting on the weight of it – and then set it down as a symbol of your entrustment of that situation to God. If you are praying for someone or something precarious and fragile you could hold something delicate (a broken eggshell, for example, or a dried flower) in your hands as a way of understanding vulnerability more deeply and offering it to God.

In Chapter 12 we thought a little about what God might 'feel' like and I described an exercise using a basket of materials – some shiny, some smooth, some soft, some hard – which asked the question, 'Which texture feels like God?' The answer would be different for everyone and one person might – in their lifetime – select a number of different textures, depending on the circumstances of their own particular journey.

This prayer uses some very tactile imagery to describe God's care:

> You are like a woollen scarf
> on a frosty day.
> You are like a soft bed
> where I may rest.
> You are like a box of treasure –
> full of surprises.
> You are like a friend
> on the end of a phone
> who's always there.
> Thank you, Lord.

'**Touch seems to be as essential as sunlight.**'

*Diane Ackerman*

The following prayer exercises are opportunities to experiment with tactile praying. But don't stop there. Develop your own ideas incorporating textures and shapes that 'speak' to you.

● ● ● ● ● ● ● ● ● ● ● ● ● ● ● ● ● ● ● ● ● ● ● ● ● ● ● ● ● ● ● ● ● ●

## Prayer exercise: **The sower**

This exercise takes Jesus' parable about a farmer sowing seed and explores it through a series of objects. You might like to prepare by reading the story in Mark's Gospel (Mark 4:3–9). Use this exercise to pray for yourself and your response to Jesus' teaching, or to pray for other people in your community. You will need a feather, a rock, a thorny twig (or a piece of barbed wire), a seed (or a packet of seeds) and a pot of compost.

'I have held many things in my hands, and I have lost them all; but whatever I have placed in God's hands, that I still possess.'

*Martin Luther*

Stand or sit within easy reach of the objects.

Take a seed and hold it in the palm of your hand. Think of all the potential that it contains and the miracle of its design.

Now think of the potential for good in your own life and/or in the community in which you live. Think of the impact Jesus' teaching has had and could have. Talk to God about this in your own words.

Set the seed down and take hold of the feather. The feather represents the birds that sometimes snatch the seed before it has a chance to grow.

Think about the things that interrupt good developments and processes – the things that distract and hinder and which prevent people and places from reaching their full potential. Talk to God about the concerns you have.

Now set down the feather and pick up the rock. Feel its hardness and its heaviness. The rock represents things that are tough – situations which are hard and where it seems unlikely that good possibilities will emerge, or that the 'seed' of God's love will ever take root. Imagine the seed trying to establish itself in this piece of rock. Pray for those places and people – or those parts of yourself – where there is resistance to God or an indifference to Jesus' teaching.

Finally take the seed again and place it in the pot of compost. Push it deep down into the nurturing soil. Hold the pot in your hands and ask God – wordlessly, or in your own words – to work in the person or place you have been praying for and to bring growth and wholeness.

*Keep your seed as a symbol of your ongoing prayer for this person or community – and remember to water it!*

• • • • • • • • • • • • • • • • • • • • • • • • • • • • • • • • • • • •

## Prayer exercise: **Clay pots**

In the book of Isaiah in the Old Testament, the prophet says to God:

> 'We are the clay, you are the potter.'
> Isaiah 64:8

This exercise explores the image of clay in the hands of a craftsman. If you have ever worked with clay you will know that it can be both wonderfully responsive and frustratingly awkward!

If you can't get hold of real clay try the air-hardening variety that many craft shops sell. You might want to cover yourself with an apron and sit at a table that you can wipe clean easily. Have a bowl of water handy to moisten the clay if it dries out in your hands and becomes crumbly.

Take a ball of clay and work it in your hands. Enjoy its texture as you squeeze and play with it. Think about how responsive it is and how easily it changes shape, but also about its resistance, its imperfections and its grittiness. Let your observations about the clay lead you into reflections about yourself – your own responsiveness and unresponsiveness, your own rough particles!

Mark the clay in some way – with your fingernail or with a knife. Spend a moment thinking about how easy it is to spoil or damage the clay. What are the things that mar God's image in you? What damage have you acquired through the circumstances of your life?

Now smooth the clay again, removing the cut or mark you made. As you experience the re-shaping of the clay, ask God to heal and restore you so that you might be all that he created you to be.

You might like to shape your clay into a simple coil or thumb pot. (Either roll the clay into a sausage and coil it into shape, or press into it with your thumb, squeezing the clay between your thumb and fingers to mould it into shape.) As you work the clay, look at your hands. Reflect on God the potter, shaping you and working in your life.

You could end by saying the words: **You are the potter, I am the clay.**

# 17 *Praying with words*

Sometimes, when we have intense experiences – either exquisitely good or unspeakably bad ones – we describe them as 'beyond words' or we use phrases like 'I cannot begin to put into words how I am feeling...' or 'words fail me'. Words are often inadequate. We cannot quite say all we want to say. Words feel too small, too flimsy or too over-used.

Sometimes our prayers are bigger than words. We want to say things to God that overspill the boundaries of language. Some people pray silently because of the limitations of words. The apostle Paul, in the letter to the Romans, talks about how God's Spirit empowers us in a way that takes us beyond language in our praying:

> ...the Spirit helps us in our weakness. We do not know what we ought to pray for, but the Spirit intercedes for us with groans that words cannot express.
>
> Romans 8:26

Some Christians pray in what is often called 'tongues' – a spontaneous prayer language that they believe God gives them as a gift. They might do this in situations when they don't know what they should pray or when words feel too constricting.

Yet words have immense power. They are the bridges between ourselves and others – the threads that connect us, one to another. Words can trigger memories, they can conjure pictures in our minds, they can wound and sting, heal or mend.

This prayer-poem describes the mystery and beyond-words-ness of prayer, and yet the very words it uses are themselves powerfully evocative:

'Words sing.
They hurt.
They teach.
They sanctify.
They were
man's first,
immeasurable
feat of magic.
They
liberated us
from
ignorance
and our
barbarous
past.'

*Leo Calvin Rosten*

My prayer
has no words,
no shape,
no form,
no face,
no feet,
no shoes.

It is delicate
as blossom,
fragile
as a butterfly's wing.

It is a dance,
a song,
a skein of silk,
a string of silver beads –
as silent as the moon,
unfathomable
as the ocean.

It has the scent of
heaven,
the certainty of
granite,

the laughter of a
child,
the stride of an
elephant.

My prayer
rises like smoke,
bubbles like a spring,
unfolds like a leaf,
penetrates
like light in a forest…
breaks, like the dawn.

To describe prayer as having 'the stride of an elephant' creates such an effective image of size and strength. Words, here, have helped us to grasp something that is essentially ungraspable – the scope and impact of our prayers.

To a parent, a baby's first words are precious. To a lover or a friend, special messages can convey love and bring comfort and joy. As the Irish playwright Samuel Beckett said, 'Words are all we have.'

Christians believe that God communicates with us through words and they describe the Bible as 'God's Word'. God entrusts the revelation of the divine character to the limitations of human language. This 'Word' is both timeless and eternally fresh.

But Jesus himself is also described as 'the Word'.

> *In the beginning was the Word, and the Word was with God, and the Word was God.*
> John 1:1

Jesus is God's ultimate message to us – God's murmur of love made flesh.

So, if words are our tools – our messengers, our declarations of divine love and our halting attempts at a response – then how can we use language that is fresh, and not tired, second-hand or clichéd? How, too, can we receive God's words to us and make them part of our thought patterns – part of the fabric of our being?

The following prayer exercises will help us with receiving words (God's to us) and employing words (ours to God).

• • • • • • • • • • • • • • • • • • • • • • • • • • • • • • • • • •

## Prayer exercise: *Lectio divina*

*Lectio divina* – or 'holy reading' – is an ancient practice that originated in the fourth century and was later embraced by Benedictine communities. Expressed simply, it is a method of reading the Bible that might be summarized in three words: *Read, Reflect, Respond.* It is a way of reading the Bible that is less about gathering information and more about letting certain words and ideas soak into the soul – and it is designed to be done slowly, without rushing.

You will need a Bible and a chair where you can be relaxed but attentive.

Choose a passage from the Bible. Colossians 3:12–17, Ephesians 3:14–21, 2 Corinthians 5:17–21, Galatians 5:13–26, Psalm 139:1–24, Psalm 8:1–9 and Isaiah 40:22–31 would all be suitable.

**Read:** Begin reading slowly, until a particular word, phrase or idea jumps out at you.

**Reflect:** Now stay with this word, phrase or idea, repeating it slowly in your mind. Imagine that you are chewing on the words, sucking every last bit of goodness out of them. One writer describes this process as 'taking a knife and fork' to the words. Gerard Hughes likens it to 'sucking a boiled sweet'. Turn the words over in your mind – searching them for every last bit of meaning.

**Respond:** When you feel you have reflected on the word or phrase and 'ingested' it fully, begin to respond in prayer – expressing to God the

'The Bible is alive, it speaks to me; it has feet, it runs after me; it has hands, it lays hold of me.'

*Martin Luther*

things you have been thinking. You may want to give thanks, or say sorry, or unburden yourself of something, or express a resolve. Having spoken to God, now spend some time in silent contemplation, allowing God space to speak to *you*.

You could conclude by saying aloud this verse from the Psalms:

> Your word is a lamp to my feet
> and a light for my path.
> Psalm 119:105

• • • • • • • • • • • • • • • • • • • • • • • • • • • • • • • • • • •

## Prayer exercise: **Cinquain poems**

This exercise gives you the chance to write a simple poem to God using a five-line cinquain (pronounced 'sink-cane') format.

Using only nine words in all (one word in the first line, two in the second, three in the third, two in the fourth and one in the fifth) the challenge is to find *the right* nine words that say exactly what you want to say – in a fresh way.

Take a pencil and a blank sheet of paper.

Focus on something specific – a Bible verse you have just read, an aspect of God's character, a particular story in the Gospels, a situation you are experiencing, a particular concern you want to bring to God in prayer.

Jot down any words or phrases that come to mind. Do this randomly and spontaneously. Don't worry at this stage about the order the words come in – or about spelling.

Now choose nine of the words that say exactly what you want to say to God and arrange them in the following order:

Word
Another word
Three more words
Then two
One

You could repeat a word for emphasis.

Here are three examples. The first reflects on the story of Jesus calming a storm (Luke 8:22–25), the second focuses on Jesus as 'bread' (see John 6:48), and the third is written by someone facing a bewildering and painful situation.

Peace!
Your voice
makes turbulent waves
become becalmed –
still.

Bread,
broken apart,
feeds my soul,
makes me
strong.

Why?
This pain –
raging, aching, raw…
Merciful God
Why?

# 18 *Praying with the imagination*

In Chapter 12 we explored the idea of praying with our whole being and giving every bit of ourselves to God in prayer. Using all of ourselves in prayer and allowing God to touch and transform all aspects of life will also involve our imaginations. Each of us is unique and we all come to God with our memories, with the information fed to us by our senses, and with all of our experiences of life – the places we've seen, the journeys we've made, the relationships we've been part of. Our imaginations are a complex tapestry of all these things: words, colours, sensations, memories – even the films we've seen and the books we've read.

Some of us mistrust our imagination, thinking of it as a realm of fairy tales and fancy, not connected to 'real life'. Others may feel they 'have no imagination'. But all of us have pictures in our heads. All of us have a fund of remembered places and scenes. Most of us can recall what it feels like to be hugged or smacked or thirsty or frightened.

How then can we use these 'pictures in our head' – these roamings of our imagination – in our praying?

The prayer exercises will give you the opportunity to use memory and imagination as a gateway into deeper kinds of praying. One will help you to visualize an encounter with Jesus in a garden. The other will take you into a scene from Luke's Gospel and invite you to imagine that you are there, participating in the drama. Don't worry if you find these exercises difficult at first. If this kind of praying or reading the Bible is unfamiliar to you it may take a while for you to get the hang of it. Ask God to guide you and to give you 'pictures in your head' that

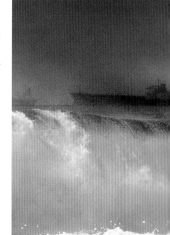

will nourish you and deepen your understanding of God and of yourself.

• • • • • • • • • • • • • • • • • • • • • • • • • • • • • • • • • • • •

## Prayer exercise: **Jesus calms the storm**

This exercise explores an incident described in Luke 8:22–25 in which Jesus' disciples experience a storm on Lake Galilee. You might like to read the story for yourself before you begin.

Sit in a chair where you can be comfortable but attentive. Become aware of your breathing and close your eyes.

Ask God to guide you in your thoughts and to help you make connections between the story and your own life.

Picture a small boat on a large lake. *If you have actually been in a boat on a lake, use this memory to help you imagine the scene.* At the moment the lake is calm.

What does the sky look like? And the water?

Think about where in the boat you are – what are your hands and feet in contact with? What does the boat's movement feel like? How does the water of the lake smell?

Picture Jesus going to sleep on a cushion on the floor of the boat, exhausted from the crowds and their demands. Bring to mind the sensation of relaxing after a draining day.

Now picture the weather changing. Notice shifts in the colour of the sky and the texture of the lake surface. Rain begins to fall, and a strong wind blows up. *Use your memories of bad weather to help you imagine a gathering storm.*

What does the wind sound like? What do the mounting waves look like? How is the boat moving in the storm?

**'I shut my eyes in order to see.'**

*Paul Gauguin*

Imagine the storm building to a point where you fear the boat will sink. Picture slippery, wet surfaces, slapping sails, water pouring in. What are you doing? Are you holding on to something? Are you bailing out water? Are you trying to change course or steer away from the bad weather or are you frozen with fear?

Jesus is still sleeping, oblivious. How does that make you feel? Are you trying to wake him? What do you expect him to do if he wakes?

Now picture Jesus as he wakes up. What is the look on his face as he stands up in the boat? What does he say when he takes in the situation?

Hear him speak to the waves and the wind, telling them to be quiet. How do his words make you feel?

Watch as the waves subside and the wind drops. Hear the silence that falls over the lake and feel the sense of calm.

What do you want to say to Jesus now?

Stay with the sense of calm and reflect on the ways in which this story resonates with your own life. What pressures and difficulties rage around you? What are the things that threaten to swamp or overwhelm you? How does the peace and calm Jesus brings alter your perception of these dangers? Which storms do you want Jesus to rebuke and silence?

You could conclude by saying aloud these words of Jesus to his disciples from John 14:27:

'Peace I leave with you;
my peace I give to you.'

• • • • • • • • • • • • • • • • • • • • • • • • • • • • • • • • • • • •

## Prayer exercise: **Walled garden**

This exercise invites you to create a space – a walled garden – in your mind (either based on a real place or places you have visited, or invented by you) and to imagine a conversation with Jesus taking place in that space.

Sit in a chair where you can be comfortable and attentive and close your eyes.

Imagine that you are outside standing in front of a door set into a high wall. You have a sense that something good awaits you on the other side of the door and that someone is inviting you to come in.

Turn the latch and open the door.

The door leads into an enclosed garden. It is a well-tended garden full of plants. Gravel paths criss-cross between beds of flowers and patches of grass and there are seats dotted around. On the walls are fruit trees and climbing roses.

In your imagination walk around the garden. What are some of the things you see? What time of year is it? What is the weather like? Which plants are in bloom? What colours and textures do you notice? Is there any human activity or wildlife in evidence?

Now imagine the sounds. When you close your eyes and listen, what do you hear?

What can you smell? Allow yourself to take in some of the scents of the garden.

Now choose one of the seats and sit down. How does the seat feel against your legs or back? Is it cold or warm? Rough or smooth? Is it in the shade or in the sun?

As you sit there, Jesus comes to sit with you. He is pleased to see you. He has been hoping you would come.

How does he greet you? Does he look at you as he sits down? How do you feel as you sit beside him in the garden?

Jesus asks you what you are thinking about – what are the things on your mind?

Imagine the things you would tell him. How does he listen? What does he say in response?

Now he asks you what you need today and what you would like him to give you. Imagine the conversation between you. Listen to what he has to say to you.

When the conversation is over you say goodbye to Jesus and walk back out of the garden, closing the door behind you as you re-enter your world. What do you bring with you from the garden?

Take a moment to reflect on how you feel.

## 19  *Praying with movement*

We have looked, in Chapters 12 to 18, at prayer that involves our senses and engages our whole selves. This chapter is about movement and the ways in which we can 'do' prayer through physical activity and the use of our bodies.

Movement in prayer is part of an ancient tradition. The Psalms urge us – over and over again – to lift up our hands in prayer.

> *Hear my cry for mercy as I call to you for help,*
> *as I lift up my hands towards your Most Holy Place.*
> Psalm 28:2

> *I will praise you as long as I live,*
> *and in your name I will lift up my hands.*
> Psalm 63:4

*Lift up your hands in the sanctuary and praise the Lord.*
Psalm 134:2

'The body is
a sacred
garment.'

*Martha Graham*

The action of lifting our hands – a reaching, stretching, embracing gesture – allows us both to express praise and openness to God and, at the same time, to 'feel' these things. Standing on tiptoes and raising our hands skywards has a naturally uplifting effect on us. We feel more hopeful, more elevated – less burdened and introspective. There is a connection between the prayer we offer, the gesture we make and the effect it has on us. We are using 'body language'.

King David took this physical praying a stage further and famously danced before God as an act of praise and thanksgiving.

*David, wearing only a linen cloth round his waist, danced with all his might to honour the Lord.*
2 Samuel 6:14

David's dancing is so wholehearted and uninhibited that his wife, spying him from a window, is thoroughly embarrassed by him!

In the movie *Chariots of Fire*, the Scottish missionary and Olympic runner Eric Liddell tells his sister that running is, for him, a way of connecting with God. He says:

'God made me fast, and when I run, I feel his pleasure.'

When Liddell runs, he celebrates the gift God has given him – as a physical act of thanksgiving – and God, in turn, communicates his sense of delight in Liddell.

Two sporty teenage boys in a youth group I was connected with spent an hour during a young people's retreat doing acrobatic routines and playing energetically on a rope swing. Afterwards they described this as prayer! By doing what they loved most – being physically active – in an attitude of offering to God, they knew, they confidently said, that they had been communicating with the one who had made them.

We may not be acrobats, dancers or Olympic runners but we can, nonetheless, express ourselves physically to God and discover the power of movement in prayer.

If nothing else we can pray by using our hands. Hands are often used as symbols of prayer, the image of 'hands together' being a readily recognized shorthand for the act of praying. Many of us will have been taught as children to put our hands palm to palm when we pray. But we can do so much more with our hands in prayer than just clasp them together, and the gestures we make can communicate a great deal – both to us and to God.

The spiritual writer Henri Nouwen has described prayer itself as the act of 'unclenching our fists'. The prayer exercise 'Open hands' will help you to explore this idea a little more.

In Chapter 10 we considered ways in which we could weave prayer into routine physical activities such as swimming or walking. One way of combining walking and prayer explicitly is to walk a labyrinth. Pathways laid out in geometric patterns called labyrinths were popular in medieval churches. (Chartres Cathedral in France has a famous labyrinth made from mosaic tiles on the floor.) Designed to be walked as an act of prayer or pilgrimage, labyrinths have become very popular again in recent years

'When I'm on a skateboard, even when I'm just rolling, I have such a freedom. That is my worship to God – just like music or dancing.'

*Christian Skater website*

and some churches and retreat centres have created their own, using stones, paint, mown grass or even gaffer tape on the floor. The slow act of walking along a twisting pathway in the company of God can be a profoundly moving experience.

Educationalists now recognize that people learn in a variety of ways and that some people – those termed 'kinaesthetic learners' – process information best through touch and movement. In other words, they learn actively, through doing things and through understanding how things *feel*. Some of us are kinaesthetic pray-ers too, finding movement extremely helpful. If you are at the fidgety end of the human spectrum and find keeping still difficult, you might discover that dancing, boulder-hopping, massage or drumming is a good way for you to pray.

• • • • • • • • • • • • • • • • • • • • • • • • • • • • • • • • • • • • •

## Prayer exercise: **Open hands**

This exercise invites you to experiment with using your hands in prayer. It uses the image of the clenched and unclenched fist as a metaphor for openness to God.

Sit comfortably in a chair and close your eyes.

In your lap, clench your fists very tightly, feeling the pressure in your fingers. Hold this position – even if it is uncomfortable.

Focus your attention on the sensation of your tightly shut hands. Ask God to reveal to you:

- ways in which you are closed to God or to other people

- grudges or negative thoughts that you might be holding on tightly to

- parts of your life where you feel stress and strain.

Now begin to relax your hands and slowly unfurl your fingers until your unclenched hands are resting in your lap, palms upwards.

Ask God to make you open to himself and his agendas in the same way that your hands are now open. Enjoy the sensation of your relaxed fingers. Spend some time thanking God for all that is good in your life.

Now open your eyes and look at your empty hands. What are the things you need? What are the qualities you lack? Where do you feel powerless or vulnerable? Where in the world are you aware of need and emptiness? Express these thoughts to God in prayer – silently or out loud.

Finally, raise your hands to God in gratitude and worship.

You could conclude by saying the words of this poem by Monica Furlong which is called 'A Prayer of Offering':

> We hold up our smallness to your greatness,
> Our fear to your love,
> Our tiny act of giving to your great generosity,
> Ourselves to you.

• • • • • • • • • • • • • • • • • • • • • • • • • • • • • • • • • • • •

## Prayer exercise: **Bear each other's burdens...**

This exercise physically enacts the image of weight-bearing to bring alive the apostle Paul's words in Galatians 6:2 about mutual support:

> Bear one another's burdens, and in this way you will fulfil the law of Christ.

**You will need to do this exercise with a partner – preferably someone of similar size – or in a larger group.**

In pairs, stand back-to-back or side-to-side, just touching. Relax and breathe deeply, becoming aware of your own and your partner's breathing rhythm.

Now move apart a little and lean against each other so that you are bearing one another's weight. (You may need to adjust your feet until you feel comfortable and secure.)

As you lean against your partner, meditate on your needs – the ways in which you need support and help, the people who support and help you. Use your awareness of your partner's strength to focus your mind on the ways in which you are dependent.

Now shift your awareness to the way in which you are bearing the weight of your partner. Feel their trust as they lean against you. Feel your strength as you are braced against them. Think about the needs of others in your family, your community and in the global community – and the ways in which you support (or *could* support) or help them.

Then, in your own time (but warning your partner first), take your weight back on your own feet and move apart.

You might like to talk about the experience together. Did you find it difficult or easy to trust each other? Did you feel safe? Are you more comfortable giving support or receiving it?

You could conclude by saying this prayer together:

> Powerful God,
> you are our strength and our refuge.
> Around us are your loving arms.
> Bless all those whose burdens we carry
> and all those who give us their loving support.
> Amen.

# 20 *Praying through creativity*

Christians believe that all human beings are made in the image of God. God is Creator – the one who brooded over the void, creating order and pattern from chaos. God is the maker of rainbows and glaciers, butterflies' wings and sand dunes. When we are creative – in however small and insubstantial a way – we mirror the creativity of God, in whose likeness we were formed. By participating in creative activities, we can glimpse the divine.

Some people feel they are 'not creative'. Many of us neglect the impulse to make things, to create beauty, to be inventive and to play. Creativity can encompass many things. We might draw, make models, do embroidery, weave fabric, carve things from wood, or do calligraphy. But simple DIY tasks can also be 'creative'. We might tile a bathroom, build a pond, plant some bulbs, paint a room. Even cooking a meal for people we love can be an act of creativity. And all these things can be a form of prayer too.

The artist Henri Matisse – though himself uncertain about his religious beliefs – said of his painting that:

> ...the essential thing is to put oneself in a frame of mind which is close to that of prayer.

How can we approach acts of creativity in a prayerful frame of mind? How can we use these moments of making things as times of communion with God? How can our art, our sewing, our DIY be a prayer?

Here are some ideas that might help you make the link between creativity and prayer:

- Approach the activity with a sense of reverence and delight.

- Thank God for the colours and textures of the materials you are working with and for your skill and the pleasure of creating something.

- Acknowledge setbacks, frustrations or a sense of limitation to God and ask God to show you inner truths through the painstaking work of creation.

- Pray, as you make things, for the people who will benefit from what you are making. Pray for those whose creativity has been stifled by hardship, poverty or abuse.

- Simply offer the time you are spending to God. Offer the process and the product. Let the whole thing be a celebration whether it has an end result or not.

We looked, in Chapter 13, at the power of visual images and at the extra dimension that seeing can bring to our life of prayer. Looking at paintings by great artists such as Michelangelo, Rembrandt or Matisse can be a deeply spiritual experience. Art can be a visual form of prayer. Paintings – like music – can sometimes 'say' what words cannot.

*'I thirst'* by Gillian Lever

Abstract artist Gillian Lever – who, in 2004, painted a series of seven large canvases based on the 'Seven Last Words of Christ from the Cross' – sees her art as visual prayers or meditations:

Working intuitively with a blank canvas involves leaping into the unknown, it is not a sure thing but it is a mysterious and wonderful thing. Sometimes a struggle, sometimes a celebration, it can be a way of honestly responding to the pain and beauty of this life's journey.

GILLIAN LEVER

*The Council of God* by Richard Kenton Webb

In Chapter 12 the prayer exercise 'Sensing God' invited us to think about colour, asking the question 'What colour is God?'

Richard Kenton Webb, a contemporary painter, had an exhibition in 2000 that was entitled 'The Colour of God'. He says this:

> What does wisdom look like? What does it feel like? What does being in the presence of the living God, Father, Son and Holy Spirit look like? It is not necessarily seeing or perhaps hearing, but feeling. If we allow colour, shape, size and movement to proclaim our whole response, then our thought is made visible. Making a painting and trusting on such lean ideas pushes you into the realm of faith.

**'Creativity is inventing, experimenting, growing, taking risks, breaking rules, making mistakes, and having fun.'**

*Mary Lou Cook*

The following prayer exercises invite you to experiment with colour and texture to express yourself to God in prayer.

As you embark on the suggested prayer exercises – or on

whatever journey of creativity you make – this prayer, attributed to Michelangelo, seems apt:

Lord,
make me see your glory
in every place.
Amen.

• • • • • • • • • • • • • • • • • • • • • • • • • • • • • • • • • • • • •

### Prayer exercise: **Prayer bowls**

This exercise is lots of fun. You will need a smooth-sided bowl of some kind (which will be undamaged by the activity), PVA glue, a glue spreader or brush, and sheets of tissue paper in assorted colours (the crinkly kind of tissue paper found in craft or gift shops – not the kind for blowing your nose on). If you retained your torn tissue from the exercise in Chapter 6, use this.

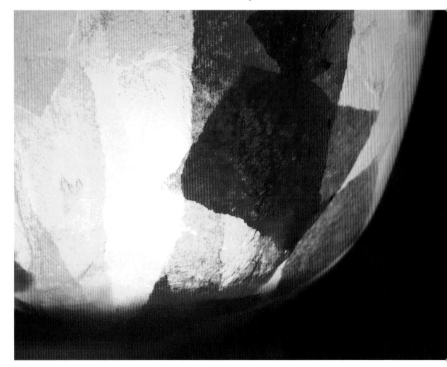

It may be wise to protect yourself with an apron and to cover any surfaces with newspaper so you can be free from worry about mess.

Spend a little time sitting quietly – stilling yourself, slowing your breathing and becoming newly conscious of God's presence with you.

Offer what you are about to do, and the time you will spend doing it, to God and ask God to bless it.

Tear the tissue paper into strips. Spread PVA glue generously *inside* the bowl and begin to line the bowl with strips of tissue paper.

You may want to choose colours symbolically to represent something in your journey with God, or you may prefer simply to choose colours that appeal to you. Remember you can mix colours (for example, red and yellow to make orange) by laying one colour on top of another. You could create blocks of colour or mingle colours together. Smooth the tissue against the side of the bowl so that it is flat and well coated in glue. Take time to enjoy the texture of the glue and the softness of the paper.

Keep going until the bowl is fully lined with no spaces in it.

You will need to leave the glue to dry for a day or so. Once it is completely dry you can peel the whole thing away from the bowl, as the PVA glue will have given the whole thing a plastic texture. You will be left with a transparent, beautiful, multi-coloured prayer bowl.

• • • • • • • • • • • • • • • • • • • • • • • • • • • • • • • • • • • • •

## Prayer exercise: **The colour of God**

This exercise is quite messy. Using paint – either poster paint (the sort children use in schools and playgroups), acrylics or oil paints – you are going to create bands of colour that articulate something of your response to God. Don't be put off if you haven't painted before. No skill in drawing is necessary. Your painting will simply be an exploration of colour and texture. Wear an apron and cover surfaces with newspaper. You could paint onto paper (lining paper from a wallpaper shop is suitable and cheap), onto board or onto one of the ready-made canvases that can be bought quite cheaply from art shops. (If you don't fancy painting you could do a similar

> '**Creativity involves breaking out of established patterns in order to look at things in a different way.**'
>
> *Edward de Bono*

exercise using collage materials such as wool, torn paper, braid or buttons.)

Spend a little time sitting quietly – stilling yourself, slowing your breathing and becoming newly conscious of God's presence with you.

Offer what you are about to do, and the time you will spend doing it, to God and ask God to bless it.

Choose a colour that appeals to you – either because it reminds you of something or 'says something' to you, or simply because you like it.

Apply it to your surface with a brush, a roller, a palette knife or your hands, creating a horizontal band. Choose whether you want to apply it thickly or thinly and whether you want a smooth or textured finish. How does the colour make you feel? Use this as a prayer.

Now add another colour above or below. You decide whether or not you want the colours to 'bleed' together. Reflect on the similarity or contrast of the two colours. Do they represent different human experiences, different aspects of God or different stages of your journey?

Keep painting until you've run out of steam! You could do one painting or several.

Before you begin to clean up, take a moment to thank God for all that the experience has taught you and spend some time enjoying what you have made, knowing that God delights in you and in the works of your hands – whatever you may think of them!

# Bibliography

David Adam, *The Rhythm of Life,* Triangle, 1996.

David Adam, *Tides and Seasons,* Triangle, 1989.

Angela Ashwin, *Woven into Prayer,* Canterbury Press, 1999.

Augustine of Hippo, *Confessions,* Oxford paperbacks, 1998.

Stephen Cottrell, *Praying through Life,* CHP, 2003.

Monica Furlong, *Prayers and Poems,* SPCK, 2004.

Richard Harries, *Prayer and the Pursuit of Happiness,* Fount, 1985.

Gerard Hughes, *God of Surprises,* DLT, 1985.

Bill Hybels, *Too Busy Not to Pray,* IVP, 1988.

Brother Lawrence, *The Practice of the Presence of God,* Hodder and Stoughton, 1989.

C. S. Lewis, *The Screwtape Letters,* Fount, 1998.

Anthony de Mello, *Sadhana: A Way to God,* Doubleday, 1984.

Henri Nouwen, *Seeds of Hope,* DLT, 1989.

John Pritchard, *How to Pray,* SPCK, 2002.

Michael Ramsey, *Be Still and Know,* Fount, 1982.

Lois Rock, *Glimpses of Heaven,* Lion, 1997.

Richard Rohr, *Everything Belongs,* Crossroad NY, 1999.

Margaret Silf, *At Sea with God,* DLT, 2003.

Margaret Silf, *Sacred Spaces,* Lion, 2001.

Margaret Silf, *Taste and See,* DLT, 1999.

Nicola Slee, *Easter Garden,* Fount, 1990.

Nicola Slee, *Praying Like a Woman,* SPCK, 2004.

William Tenny-Brittian, *Prayer for People who Can't Keep Still,* Chalice Press, 2005.

Philip Yancey, *Finding God in Unexpected Places,* Hodder and Stoughton, 1995.

p. 15 For more information on labyrinths and a 'virtual labyrinth' see the site www.labyrinth.org.uk.

# Picture Acknowledgments

AKG-Images/Zooid Pictures Ltd: p. 85.

Alamy: pp. 8 (Mediacolor's), 47 (archivberlin Fotoagentur GmbH), 53 (EggImages), 81 (Roger Coulam), 90 (Huw Jones), 109 (Mark Higgins), 114 (David Sanger Photography), 116 (Colin Wood).

Ardea London Ltd: p. 38 (Jim Zipp).

Digital Vision: pp. 13, 25, 42.

Rivers Fiji: p. 113.

Gillian Lever: p. 120.

Lion Hudson: pp. 33 (David Townsend), 67 (Nicholas Rous), 77, 88.

Frank Mayfield: pp. 10, 34–35, 59, 62, 101.

George Mayfield: p. 24

Sue Mayfield: pp. 68, 78.

Tim Mayfield: pp. 17, 31, 75.

Andy Rous: pp. 14, 22, 28, 41, 50, 54, 63, 66, 79, 86, 92, 95, 97, 99, 103, 105, 122.

Nicholas Rous: p. 20–21, 111.

Richard Webb: p. 121.